THE CAPTURE OF DAMIETTA

UNIVERSITY OF PENNSYLVANIA
DEPARTMENT OF HISTORY

*TRANSLATIONS AND REPRINTS FROM THE
ORIGINAL SOURCES OF HISTORY*

Edited by JOHN L. LAMONTE

First Series

Six Volumes. Details Available on Request.

Second Series

Volume 1. SELECTIONS FROM THE WRITINGS OF ZWINGLI. Edited by SAMUEL MACAULEY JACKSON. *Out of print.*

Volume 2. THE MERCHANT ADVENTURERS OF ENGLAND. Edited by W. E. LINGELBACH. *Out of print.*

Volume 3. THE HISTORY OF THE LANGOBARDS BY PAUL THE DEACON. Translated by WILLIAM DUDLEY FOULKE.

Third Series

Volume 1. FULCHER OF CHARTRES: CHRONICLE OF THE FIRST CRUSADE. Translated by MARTHA EVELYN MCGINTY.

Volume 2. THE CAPTURE OF DAMIETTA BY OLIVER OF PADERBORN. Translated by JOHN J. GAVIGAN.

The Capture of Damietta

BY OLIVER OF PADERBORN

Translated by

JOHN J. GAVIGAN

Philadelphia

UNIVERSITY OF PENNSYLVANIA PRESS

London: Geoffrey Cumberlege
Oxford University Press

1948

Copyright 1948

UNIVERSITY OF PENNSYLVANIA PRESS

Manufactured in the United States of America

FOREWORD

IN SELECTING *The Capture of Damietta* by Oliver of Paderborn for inclusion in the "Translations and Reprints," two major considerations influenced the editor. In the first place, the Fifth Crusade is one of the most interesting and least-known episodes in medieval history, and Oliver's is the most detailed account left by any participant therein. Secondly, the mind of Oliver is well revealed in his work, and it seemed most desirable to make available in translation this very human document from the opening of the thirteenth century. We are well informed regarding the psychology of the participants in the First Crusade, but we know much less about those in the following century.

The Fifth Crusade has an interest shared by none of the other crusades. None started out more bravely or accomplished more quickly the goal set. The grand strategy of the thirteenth-century crusades was to attack Egypt and force the return of Jerusalem as the price of restoring to the Sultan of Egypt cities in his own land which could be captured more readily than could Jerusalem. The increasing naval strength of the western states gave them an advantage in a campaign which could be conducted largely by sea. The Third Crusade had demonstrated the difficulties of campaigning in Palestine; in both the Fourth and the Fifth Crusades the strategy planned out was a naval attack on Egypt which would reduce the Sultan to surrendering Jerusalem to buy off the attackers. In its avowed aim the Fifth Crusade was conspicuously successful. Even before Damietta was captured, the Sultan offered the return of Jerusalem; after the city had been taken by the Christians he offered the return of all the former Kingdom of Jerusalem with the exception of the territories east of the Dead Sea. This was all that the crusaders could have hoped for; John de Brienne spoke for the great majority when he advocated the acceptance of Al Kamil's terms. But the crusade had passed out of the control of the secular leaders. Pelagius of Albano, the Papal Legate, insisted on continuing the war with the hope of reducing Cairo itself. Nothing could alter the determination of the proud prelate to carry on the war to the end, thus reaping greater glory for the Church. Pelagius and Honorius, in whose name he spoke, both preferred the glory of a victorious crusade to the solid benefits of a reëstablished Kingdom of Jerusalem. The crusaders from the West never seemed to understand fully the problems or the position of the Syrian Franks; during the Third Crusade they took opposite positions, and they were only further apart in the Fifth.

More than any other crusade, the Fifth was a Papal venture. Many of the soldiers involved were Papal mercenaries; the leadership was entrusted neither to kings (as in the Second and Third) nor to barons (as in the First and Fourth) but was kept securely in the hands of the Papal Legate. As never before, the Church insisted on maintaining its own military leadership and command. It was this ecclesiastical command, which overruled the more practical counsels of the lay leaders, that was responsible for the utter debacle of the crusade. The failure of the crusade must be laid squarely on the shoulders of Pelagius. True, he may have been misled by the unfulfilled promises of Frederick II, but that is not enough to exculpate him from the blame for the fiasco.

This ecclesiastical insistence on military command seems to me to indicate a change in Papal policy towards the crusades. No longer were the Popes interested fundamentally in rescuing the Holy Sepulchre and the Holy Land of Jerusalem; they sought instead to be managers of a successful military movement which would redound to the glory of Rome and the Church. Pelagius was the ideal instrument for carrying out such a policy; unfortunately for himself and the Papacy, he overplayed his hand. Even Oliver, who supported Pelagius and the Church party blindly and loyally, could not but remark that King John, "reflecting more deeply on the matter, wisely showed that the proposal so often proffered by the enemy ought to be accepted" (p. 83).

As virtually nothing has been written in English about the Fifth Crusade, it seemed the more desirable that a good original narrative thereof should be translated and offered to the English-speaking public.

Oliver's work is, however, valuable in another respect, for it is a window into the mind and soul of the thirteenth-century crusader. As we can see the ordinary little man of the First Crusade in the Chronicle of Fulcher of Chartres, so we can see the simple crusader of the Fifth in the book of Oliver. Both Fulcher and Oliver were clerics who participated in the crusade with simple piety and religious enthusiasm. Paul Rousset, in his *Les Origines et les Caractères de la Première Croisade* (Geneva-Neuchatel, 1945), has studied the psychology of the men who went on the First Crusade or lived in Europe at that time. Whatever the motives of some of the leaders such as Bohemond, there can be no question that the common soldiers were inspired by religious zeal. It is commonly recognized that the later crusades were much less religious than the earlier. Villehardouin and Joinville, the most familiar thirteenth-century crusade historians, both write as laymen dealing with secular campaigns; Frederick II certainly was moved by no considerations of religion. We are apt to forget that religion was still the compelling force in the minds of many of the humbler participants.

This we can see in Oliver. Not the prowess of the Franks but the will of God gave them victory; not poor command and unreasonable pride but the excessive sinfulness of the crusaders brought disaster on their heads. To Oliver the crusaders were the soldiers of God, blindly carrying out His inscrutable will. At times the excessive piety of our author becomes exceedingly boring and we could wish that he indulged in less biblical quotation and gave us more detailed descriptions of the persons and events portrayed; but to cut out any of his pious discourses would be to change his sense of values and to lose the picture of his mind and emotions. Miracles abound; the prayers of the clergy and the miraculous power of the True Cross are as effective as the deeds of the warriors, and all is according to God's will. Here we see laid bare the soul of a pious and deeply religious cleric of the thirteenth century, a master of arts, a bishop of Paderborn, a cardinal-bishop of Saint Sabina.

Oliver's natural interest in religion causes him to indulge in a long excursus on the various Christian sects he encountered in the East. He evidently made some study of Islam, though he did not completely comprehend the teachings of Mohammed. But it is interesting that he feels that the Moslems were rather heretics than infidels. Nevertheless Hell awaits them all, for heresy is as bad as paganism.

At times Oliver reaches certain heights of descriptive power. One can almost smell the stench of the dead bodies at Damietta or feel the cold wet of the partially inundated camp. On the other hand, his geography is not overly clear. The map that accompanies this translation is meant to show only the principal places connected with the Fifth Crusade; many of the smaller towns and villages in Lower Egypt mentioned by Oliver no longer exist and cannot be found on modern maps, while others are impossible of differentiation on a small scale map. Raamses, which Oliver locates incorrectly in his text, is placed in approximately the position given in the Ortelius *Atlas* of 1573. In this connection, a word concerning the coin in the lower right hand corner of the map is appropriate. It is drawn from a denier struck by John de Brienne at Damietta in 1219–21. It was given to the editor by Dr. Dorothy H. Cox, and is one of the coins described in her *Tripolis Hoard of French Seignorial and Crusader's Coins* (American Numismatic Society, *Notes and Monographs*, No. 59 [1933]).

Father John J. Gavigan, who prepared the translation and notes, comes to Oliver from a background of classical and medieval Latin study. He is the author of "The Syntax of the *Gesta Francorum*" (*Language*, XIX, iii, Supplement [Sept. 1943]) and assistant professor of classics at Villanova College. As a concession to his philological interest, Appendix B of this work discusses briefly the language and syntax employed by Oliver. Dr. Gavigan's classical soul has at times been horrified by the free translation in which the editor has on occasion indulged in an attempt to simplify Oliver's somewhat turgid style. On the whole, however, the translation follows closely the exact phraseology of Oliver's text, both in its moments of fine description and in its more pedestrian passages. The diligence with which Dr. Gavigan has run down obscure persons and places mentioned in the text is no less evident than the extreme care devoted to the translation itself. The text is of course entirely uncut and unabridged. It is Oliver's book as he wrote it.

University of Pennsylvania JOHN L. LAMONTE
November 1946

CONTENTS

	Page
FOREWORD	v
INTRODUCTION	1
THE CAPTURE OF DAMIETTA	11
APPENDIX A. CONCLUDING SECTION OF THE DARMSTADT MANUSCRIPT	96
APPENDIX B. BRIEF LINGUISTIC COMMENTARY	98
BIBLIOGRAPHY	101
INDEX	105

Map

THE LEVANT AND THE NILE DELTA, XIII CENTURY *Drawing by Robert E. LaMont*	xii

Nihil obstat

Joseph A. M. Quigley
Censor Librorum

Philadelphiae, die 2ª Novembris, 1946

Imprimatur

✠ D. Cardinalis Dougherty
Archiepiscopus Philadelphiensis

Philadelphiae, die 7ª Novembris, 1946

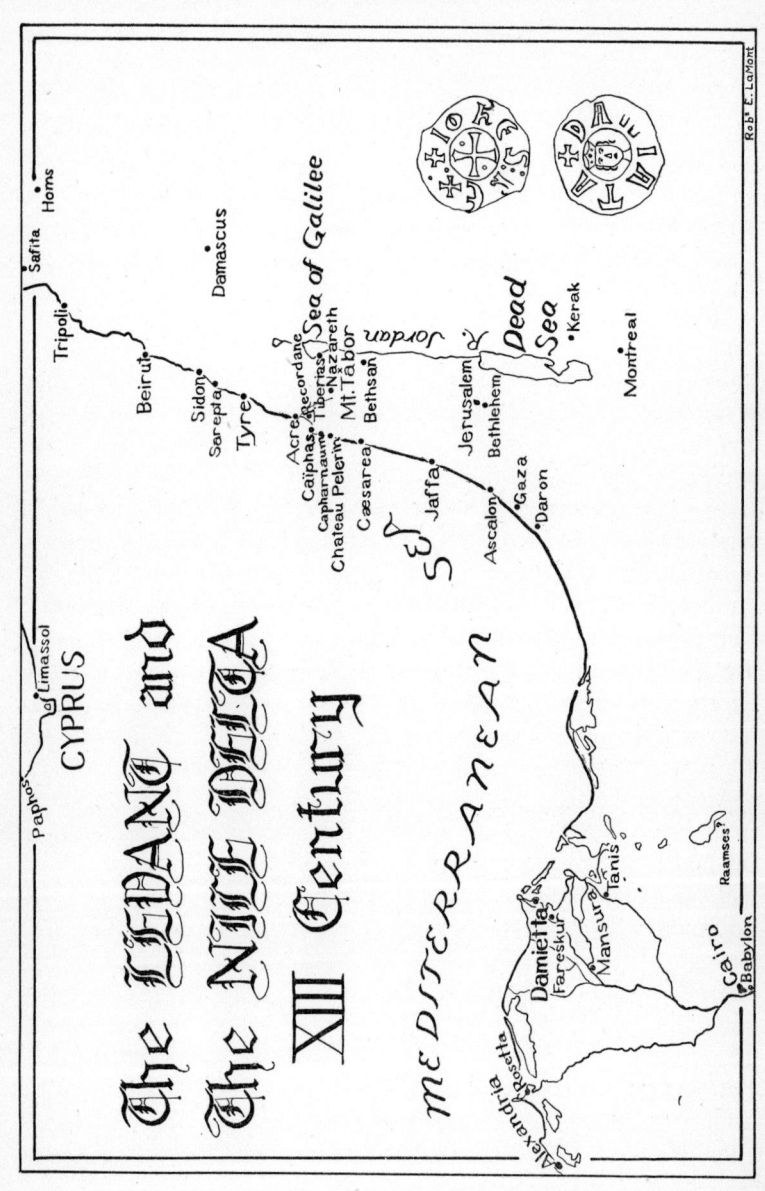

INTRODUCTION

OLIVER'S EARLY LIFE

One of the earliest acts of the pontificate of Honorius III had been to make in 1216 an appeal to the Christians of Europe for a crusade.[1] Country after country took up the summons. Hungary under King Andrew II, Germany under Duke Leopold of Austria, and the Scandinavian countries under Duke Casimir of Pomerania and Prince Sigurd of Norway were most zealous in their response. Emperor Frederick II of Germany, however, the man the whole world expected to be the leader for the crusade, obtained a deferment because of strife in his kingdom. Despite many troubles, the crusaders advanced, and found in Acre the three kings of Hungary, Cyprus, and Jerusalem as their leaders. Unity of direction was lacking, and strife and distrust were the result. In spite of the constant efforts of Honorius and the initial success of the Christians, Damietta was lost permanently, and the crusade was looked upon by all as another sad failure.

Among those who had accompanied the pilgrims were prelates from every land. Cardinals, bishops, and priests joined their aid to the labors of the soldiers. One of these, Oliver of Paderborn, who had preached the crusade in the province of Cologne, found opportunity to perpetuate in writing the experiences of the Fifth Crusade. This writing, of which the first English translation is here offered, is called the *Historia Damiatina*. In addition, Oliver devoted his pen to the geography and history of the Holy Land. Three other works, to be mentioned later, were devoted to this. Further, at least ten letters from Oliver's pen are still extant.

Of his birth, childhood, and early education we have no knowledge. His name appears for the first time in 1196 as an episcopal

---

[1] See Bréhier, *L'Église et l'Orient: Les Croisades*, p. 190. Fuller details about works cited here and elsewhere are given in the Bibliography.

witness in a quarrel between the diocese of Paderborn and the monastery of Helmarhaus.² Since the witnesses were members of the cathedral chapter of Paderborn, and since these canons were almost exclusively from the nobility, we may safely assume that Oliver belonged to a noble family of the diocese. However, in addition to the accident of birth, he appears to have been fitted for the rank of canon by traits of character which can be observed in his writings. His *Historia Damiatina* shows on nearly every page that he was a man of piety, religious zeal, and simple unwavering faith.

He seems to have been outstanding intellectually in his young manhood, and he merited the title *magister*, which at that time was used to mark out one of exceptional learning.³ In 1200 we find him as headmaster and teacher of theology at the grammar school of Paderborn. He held this post but a short time, however, for in September 1201 the Archbishop of Cologne asked him to fill the professor's chair in the cathedral school left vacant by the famed scholastic Rudolph. To one of Oliver's ability such an opportunity must have been a delight, for Cologne was then at the height of her power, the acknowledged leader of all German cities and a center of influence and culture. Its political life, however, was in a state of violent turmoil. Philip of Swabia and Otto of Brunswick were engaged in their quarrel over the imperial throne, and the clerics were drawn into the struggle, most of them favoring Otto in deference to the opinion of Pope Innocent III. Oliver kept favorable impressions of the city, as appears from a later flattering reference made to it.⁴

Oliver was in Paris in 1207, although it is not known how long he had been there in that year. During his stay in that city he attended its famous university, which the whole civilized world admired and praised for its teaching.

Just at this time the Pope began to unfold his cherished plans for a new crusade.⁵ It seemed an unfavorable moment for such a project, for Germany was worn out by the struggle between the Welfs

---

² Hoogeweg, *Die Schriften des . . . Oliver*, p. ix. This work contains all of Oliver's works and a study of the author. It has been the most valuable secondary work used in preparing the present Introduction.

³ *Ibid.*, p. xi.

⁴ *See* p. 49 and note 3, p. 49.

⁵ Bréhier, *op. cit.*, p. 179.

and the Hohenstaufen; France was involved on one side with the rapidly spreading Albigensian heresy, while on the other she was keeping herself on guard against trouble with England. Yet the new crusade found enthusiastic support, and Innocent felt a revival of his hope that perhaps Jerusalem would at last return to the hands of the Christians. In a bull of January 30, 1208, he requested the Bishop of Geneva and the Abbot of Bonnevaux to see that the Bishop of Grenoble bestow on Oliver a small church in Epernay for some services which he had rendered. Oliver subsequently returned to Cologne, where he remained between 1209 and 1213, although it is not known how he was employed. In the spring of 1213 a new field of activity opened to him, when from Pope Innocent letters were sent out to all Christendom, begging for the liberation of the Holy Sepulchre. Men of zeal and eloquence were named to preach the Cross throughout the lands of Europe. In company with the Dean of Bonn, Oliver was assigned to the province of Cologne, and during the years 1214-15 he labored in Lüttich, Namur, Brabant, Flanders, Geldt, Utrecht, and Friesland. Two letters that he wrote at this time give us a clear picture of his work as a preacher. Success attended him all along his way. The Frisians in particular received his message with an affection amounting almost to veneration.

In the midst of his preaching Oliver was sent to Rome to act as representative for the archbishopric of Cologne at the great Lateran Council of 1215, which decreed among many other points that the crusaders should depart for the Holy Land on June 1, 1217. By April 10, 1216, Oliver was again in Lüttich, ready to resume his work of preaching the crusade, but we cannot trace his activities during the year that followed. When the day appointed for the departure drew near, Oliver joined the crowds of pilgrims who thronged to Marseilles, journeying across the sea to the Holy Land, arriving in July or August, probably at Acre.

THE FIFTH CRUSADE, AND OLIVER'S WORKS

The period that ensued has been described for us in full by Oliver himself. In addition to a detailed account of events, he has unwittingly given us a clearer insight into his own character, allowing us to discover more than a trace of prudence, moderation, diligence, zeal, gratitude, loyalty, humility, and trust in God. Prudence and moderation appeared in his counsel to the crusaders, though his modesty prevented him from naming himself as the propounder of such wise advice.

Merely to glance at his narrative of the crusade would be to realize it was the work of a diligent and painstaking man. The greatest part, at any rate, of the *Historia Damiatina* was written during the crusade itself and immediately after, therefore between 1217 and 1222. This is evident from the use of both present and future tenses that appears through the work. It adds greater vividness to the narrative in many places. That the last section of the work was completed in Egypt is possible, but cannot be determined accurately. The last dated event is September 1222, when a summons was made for a council to be held at Verona on November 11 of that year.

When we consider that Oliver wrote three works in addition to the *Historia Damiatina* while in Egypt, without neglecting the duties of his position as cleric, we cannot doubt his energy and application. From the outset his zeal was clearly apparent, yet nowhere was it more evident than in his efforts to convert the Sultan and his followers from Islam to Christianity. There are in this episode indications of gratitude; Oliver appreciated the Sultan's magnanimity toward the Christian captives, and his desire to offer a gift in recompense for the kindness could find no more perfect gift than that of the true faith.[6] The Sultan, however, remained a staunch adherent of Islam.

Loyalty to Christ, and consequently to all those who act in His name, led Oliver to speak of Cardinal Pelagius in a manner somewhat different from that of other historians.[7] Where most observers saw ambition and a selfish craving for power, Oliver saw God's representative; his words seemed the words of divine wisdom, and

---

[6] Grousset has pointed out, however, that this kindness was not entirely disinterested. The Sultan realized that further contingents of crusaders were due to arrive shortly. He was unwilling to incur their further displeasure by a harsh treatment of their comrades. (*Histoire des Croisades*, III, 243.)

[7] Some historians have blamed Pelagius as the chief cause of the crusade's failure. This has never secured universal acceptance, however, among either medieval or modern authors.

as such could not conceivably find criticism from Oliver. Nowhere do we see the picture of Pelagius as an intolerant, arrogant tyrant; rather we find everywhere phrases lauding the skill of the Legate, his wisdom and zeal, his efficiency and ability. With such an attitude toward the Cardinal, Oliver would obviously find little to admire in John of Brienne, since the two leaders were opposite both in temperament and in outlook; and there is more than a hint of criticism in Oliver's allusions to John.

Not confining his criticisms to individuals, Oliver repeatedly points out weaknesses among the crusaders as a group. On page after page we read such phrases as: "It was the punishment of sin"; "Lust of the eyes made thieves of many"; "Since the defenders acted negligently"; evidences that in spite of his love of the ideal, he is by no means blind to reality. The deplorable sinfulness of the Christians seems in Oliver's opinion to be the cause of the army's various losses, rather than any superiority on the part of the Saracens—though once or twice he is compelled to admit that they are skilled and practised fighters. In the midst of gloom and desolation, however, Oliver invariably derives solace from the mention of the Germans, and particularly the Frisians: "Most praise was deservedly given to that obedient and energetic nation, who from the beginning attacked Damietta with great courage, and considered no position either humble or lowly." [8] The Templars too receive their meed of praise; among many similar expressions we find: "the army of the Temple, which is usually first to assemble, was the last to retreat." [9]

In every occurrence of the ill-fated crusade, Oliver could perceive a manifestation of divine Providence. "By the plan of the Holy Ghost"; "Let the victory be ascribed to the Son of God alone"; "through the intervention of His mercy, the miracle shone forth," and like expressions recur constantly throughout the narrative, obviously the sincere utterance of a mind accustomed to consider God's presence as a vivid reality. He considered himself, therefore, all the more obliged to persevere to the very end and to remain faithful to the crusader's vow. What excuse, he says, can they have before the Judge Who cannot be bribed or deceived, if they receive

[8] *See* p. 92.
[9] *See* p. 43.

His benefits, but neglect their pledged duties? What rewards could those faithful on the other hand expect who came from distant lands and persevered in a holy war? Even though success has not crowned their efforts, he continues, will the Lord not be pleased with the sacrifices they have made in leaving home and loved ones for His sake? The crushing loss of Damietta seemed to have no dampening effect on his ardor, for he could still write to Al-Kamil and the "Doctors of Egypt" to persuade them to accept Christianity.

In some instances Oliver's views display a decided tendency toward credulity. He is inclined to interpret slight successes as miracles, and in his description of the apparitions in Frisia this credulity is quite apparent.[10] A great profusion of scriptural references indicates familiarity with the written word of God; drawn in many cases from the less familiar portions of both Old and New Testaments, they are singularly appropriate choices, and seem to flow as naturally from Oliver's pen as words of his own fashioning. Yet his interest in divine things did not impede his actions in a field requiring skill of a practical type, for we know that it was Oliver who designed and supervised the erection of that massive tower of destruction: "Such a work of wood had never before been erected upon the water."[11] It is a point deserving of mention, too, that it is not Oliver who tells us the designer of this medieval machine; he writes with commendable modesty the simple words: "with the Lord showing us how, and providing an architect." Jacques de Vitry is the one who gives us the name of the skillful engineer.

From a literary standpoint the *Historia Damiatina* deserves a brief consideration. First, its author is clearly one who has spared no pains to include all necessary information. In the descriptions of battles especially there is a wealth of interesting detail. We are able to feel the heat of the scorching Egyptian sun, to see the gleam of helmet and sword, the flash of Greek fire, the shower of destructive arrows; our senses recoil from the horrors of a city stricken by pestilence, of a battlefield strewn with dead, of a futile, unprepared, disgraceful retreat. Numerous digressions, in

[10] *See* p. 21.
[11] *See* p. 25.

which we are taken away from the scene of battle, prove that the author had some knowledge of Saracen practices and beliefs, though he was ignorant of Arabic. It is also a matter of wonder that a man of Oliver's intelligence and education would make such little use of classical allusions. Only once do we find a definite reference: Oliver cites an incident told by Curtius Rufus in his history of Alexander the Great.[12] There are two other references to Alexander which may be from the same source,[13] and one to Julius Caesar[14] which may be based on Suetonius, though probably mediately.

The language is heavily flavored by the Latinity of the Vulgate.[15] Usually it is sufficiently clear, but occasionally an expression occurs that is involved, clumsy, or ambiguous.

We find frequent rhetorical apostrophes, outpourings of a heart that bemoaned the tragedies sent by God, and longed to stir the sluggish to action.

Oliver's works other than the *Historia Damiatina* may be mentioned here more briefly:

1. *Descriptio Terre Sancte*. Oliver felt that this geographical description would serve as a useful companion to his other works which dealt with the history of the Holy Land. It is very unoriginal, and is copied for the most part from the so-called Eugesippus-Fretellus. Hoogeweg assigns it provisionally to the year 1220, when the Christian army spent much time in inactivity after the capture of Damietta.

2. *Historia de Ortu Jerusalem et Eius Variis Eventibus*. This begins with Adam and closes with the Crusade of 1096–99 which captured the Holy City from the Mohammedans. In fact, however, it is a history of the Jews from the Creation till the capture of the city by Titus in 70. Then follows merely a list of emperors—Roman, Greek, and German. The chief sources are the Historical Books of the Old Testament and the *Historia Scholastica* of Petrus Comes-

[12] *See* p. 23.
[13] *See* pp. 58, 82.
[14] *See* p. 82.
[15] A brief discussion of the language is presented in Appendix B, pp. 98–100.

tor. After he has come to Claudius, Oliver's list of emperors is taken (perhaps mediately) from Saint Jerome and Paul the Deacon. Several chapters, however, seem original, and a few points are borrowed from further sources.

3. *Historia Regum Terre Sancte.* The first part, up to Chapter 24, is based on the *Historia Hierosolymitana* of Fulcher of Chartres in the second edition, which reached up to 1124. The next part is based on William of Tyre, beginning at Book 13 of William, and continuing up to Chapter 89 of Oliver's work. After this, Oliver apparently found other sources, which seem to have been utilized by *l'Estoire d'Eracles* also, which in many places shows a surprising similarity to the narrative of Oliver. The work finally describes the attempts of Pope Innocent III to launch a crusade, and the Lateran Council of 1215. This leads up to the Crusade of 1217 which Oliver describes at length in the *Historia Damiatina,* his most important work. The *Historia Regum* was written during the siege of Damietta in 1219–20 in a first redaction, and seems to have appeared in 1222 in a later redaction, designed to end where the *Historia Damiatina* begins.

The ten surviving letters of Oliver date from June 1214 to 1224. Four were written in Egypt. Letter 3, to the Archbishop and clergy of Cologne, describes the events of the crusade from November 3, 1217, to the end of August 1218. Letter 4, written near Damietta on September 14, 1218, to the clergy and councilors of Frisia, praises the Frisian crusaders' bravery, sacrifice, and fidelity. Letter 5, written in September 1222 to the Sultan of Egypt, asks him to accept Christianity and restore the Holy Land. Letter 6, written at the same time to the "Doctors of Egypt," tries to convince them of the divinity of Christ.

The letters are important for the *Historia Damiatina* because two of them, written from Egypt, are the source for the first part of that work. These two letters, sent by Oliver to Germany, were united to form the first section, which deals with the crusade of the King of Hungary and with the expedition that captured Damietta in 1219. To this certain additions were made, explaining points of history, geography, and culture not directly concerned with the crusade. Finally, sections were added that described the events of 1220 to 1222, and thus a unified history was completed after certain adjustments had been made by the author.

OLIVER'S LIFE AFTER THE FIFTH CRUSADE

The failure of the crusade struck a heavy blow to Oliver's deepest ambition. He wasted no time, however, on fruitless lamentations, but returned at once to his old work in Germany. On February 16, 1222, he preached a Lenten sermon in Cologne. Pope Honorius had already sent out an appeal for yet another crusade, and Oliver took up his former activity as a preacher, though we have no record that he was officially designated as such. Between February 1222 and September 1223, our only record of him is a letter that he wrote which indicates his presence in Frisia at this time, and mentions a visit to his friend the Abbot Emo at his monastery of Wittewierum.

An unfortunate incident now occurred at Paderborn, the result of the death of Bishop Bernard III on March 28, 1223. Two men were suggested for election as his successor: Oliver, and Henry von Brokel, prior of the monastery of Busdorf. Much strife arose over the election, chiefly because the von Brokel family, influential for years in the diocese, brooked no opposition to their candidate, and resorted to violence to insure his choice. An appeal to Rome finally brought approval to Oliver, but the affair was not definitely settled for many years. During part of this troubled time, Oliver stayed with Count Henry of Schwerin in Nordhausen, aiding him in a controversy with Waldemar of Denmark.

After this, he took up in earnest the preaching of the crusade, beginning on May 15. On June 1 he visited his old friend Emo at his monastery. On the Monday after Pentecost, Oliver set out again for the east of Germany, but on his journey he received a summons to Cologne, and in answer to this he abandoned his preaching for a time. Though the meeting at Cologne to which he had been summoned did not take place, Oliver was able to meet the Papal Legate, Cardinal Conrad, and was able to advance the cause of his friend Emo, who was involved in a dispute with Prior Herdericus of Schildwolde.

Oliver returned to his preaching, and found things by no means propitious to his cause. Repeated floods had brought desolation and famine to Frisia, and men were little inclined to hear invitations for another foreign journey. Private warfare was rife and the time was definitely inauspicious, but Oliver was none the less able to muster some soldiers for a new attempt.

Oliver was confirmed as Bishop of Paderborn by a letter from Honorius which arrived April 7, 1225. In July, Oliver proceeded to San Germano to receive his regalia from Emperor Frederick II, who had at last agreed to support the new crusade. Upon this occasion Oliver was obliged to borrow sixty-five silver marks in the name of the cathedral chapter of Paderborn.

Very little is known of Oliver's work as bishop, for he held the office for a short time only, and was away from the diocese for a considerable portion of it. One fact has come down to us by a document coming from Honorius: At Oliver's request, an indulgence of forty days was granted to all who visited the cathedral at Paderborn on the anniversary of its consecration. Shortly after, on September 18, Oliver signed a papal bull for Padua with his new title: Cardinal-Bishop of Saint Sabina. Honorius announced this appointment to the cathedral chapter of Paderborn on September 27.

The next mention of Oliver shows him as mediator between Emperor Frederick and the Curia, in a dispute that arose over the filling of a vacant diocese in Italy. Oliver was able to bring about a compromise; he also persuaded Frederick to write a letter to the Frisians expressing his gratitude for their brave deeds at Damietta, and fixing the date of the next departure for August 1227. Oliver now disappears from our sight; only a few letters bearing his signature remain, the latest of which is dated August 9, 1227. On September 18, Johann Halgrin was appointed Cardinal-Bishop of Saint Sabina. We conclude that Oliver had died some time between August 9 and September 18, 1227. He was buried in Italy.

THE CAPTURE OF DAMIETTA

HERE begins the history of Damietta whereat Master Oliver, compiler of this work and preacher of the Holy Cross, was undoubtedly present.

FOREWORD

"Let Mount Sion rejoice, and let the daughters of Juda be glad because of Thy judgments, O Lord. Sing ye to the Lord for He hath done great things"; [1] writing and preaching, let them announce the wonders of the Lord [2] Who hath commanded His sanctified ones and hath called His strong ones in His wrath, them that exult not in their own strength, "not in the works of justice which they themselves have done," [3] but in the glory of His majesty, Who is blessed in all things in eternity. For "the land whence arose the bread that came down from heaven" [4] in the place of His birth has been cut off by the sword, and by many fortifications which perfidious men occupy; "the stones of this land are the place of sapphires" [5] because it was the possession of the patriarchs, the nursling of the prophets, the teacher of the apostles, the mother of faith. "The clods of it are gold," [6] because the guardians of religion have clung together by charity and have never failed therein. Freed at last after many groans and frequent sighs, it now exults in hope; and trusting in the goodness of its deliverer, rejoicing, it will rejoice when "the rod of sinners has been taken away from the lot of the

---

[1] Psalms 47:12. All quotations from the Old Testament are made as closely as possible according to the Douay Version. Those from the New Testament are modeled upon the edition of the Confraternity of Christian Doctrine, Paterson, 1941.
[2] Isaias 13:3.
[3] Titus 3:5.
[4] Romans 1:25; Job 28:5; John 6:33.
[5] Job 28:6.
[6] Job 28:6.

just."[7] Indeed what we have seen and heard and have truly understood, we write to all who are orthodox without any admixture of falsity, so that whatever merit there is may appear to the praise of God, and in gratitude to Him.

CHAPTER 1

In the year 1217, when the truce of the Christians and Saracens [1] had expired, in the first general passage after the Lateran Council,[2] a large army of the Lord assembled in Acre, with the three kings of Jerusalem,[3] Hungary,[4] and Cyprus,[5] who, not bearing with them the mystic gifts, offered one not at all worthy of memory. The Duke of Austria [6] was there, and the Duke of Meran [7] with many

---

[7] Psalms 124:3.

[1] The truce which expired in 1217 was one made with Saphadin by either Aymeri de Lusignan or John d'Ibelin when Regent of Jerusalem.

[2] The Fourth Lateran Council (the twelfth oecumenical) of 1215, was the greatest of the Middle Ages and is sometimes referred to simply as *the* Lateran Council. It was summoned by Pope Innocent III (+1216). It defined the Incarnation and other mysteries against the Albigensians; condemned the errors of Joachim on the Trinity; recognized the second place of the Patriarch of Constantinople; forbade the establishment of new religious orders; legislated against pluralism; and stated the requirement of at least annual confession and communion.

[3] John of Brienne, King of Jerusalem, 1210–25; Emperor of Constantinople, 1228–37. He received the crown of Jerusalem when he married Marie de Montferrat in 1210 and lost it in 1225 when his daughter Isabelle married Frederick II. He was military leader and hero of the expedition against Damietta but was absent for a time owing to his difficulties with Pelagius (*see* pp. 61–3), and while he was advancing claims to the throne of Armenia.

[4] Andrew II, King of Hungary, 1203–35, son of Bela III and Margaret, Princess of France. He left the crusade at the beginning of 1218. (*See* p. 17, n. 2.) Later (1233) he became the husband of Yolanda Courtenay, Empress of Constantinople.

[5] Hugh of Lusignan, King of Cyprus, 1205–18, son of Aymeri and Eschive d'Ibelin. He married Alice of Champagne-Jerusalem, daughter of Isabelle of Jerusalem and Henry of Champagne, who, after Hugh's death, played an important role in the politics of the Latin states.

[6] Leopold VI, the Glorious, Duke of Austria, 1198–1230, who fought in Spain in 1212, but arrived too late for the famous battle of Las Navas de Tolosa (*See* Oliver's *Historia regum*, 115, 357 [ed. Hoogeweg]).

[7] Otto VII, duke of Meran, 1204–34, belonged to a particularly illustrious family. His parents were Berthold IV, Duke of Meran (+1204), and Agnes

THE CAPTURE OF DAMIETTA

companions and men of noble birth, and the great soldiery of the Teutonic king. There were present pilgrim bishops, the Archbishop of Nicosia,[8] Raab,[9] Erlau,[10] Hungary,[11] Bayeux,[12] Bamberg,[13] Zeitz,[14] Münster,[15] and Utrecht;[16] with them was a powerful and noble man, Lord Walter of Avesnes,[17] who, returning in the spring crossing, left forty soldiers in the service of the Holy Land, and provided them with funds sufficient for a year. The Bavarians conducted themselves insolently, and contrary to the law of pilgrims, by destroying the gardens and orchards of the Christians, even casting religious out of their hospices; when this did not satisfy them, they killed the Christians. The Duke of Austria, like a Catholic prince, fought for Christ throughout.

---

of Groitsch-Rochlitz (+1194 or 1195). Otto married Beatrice of Hohenstaufen, Heiress of Bergundy. Brothers of Otto were Henry, Margrave of Istria, 1204–09; Berthold V, Patriarch of Aquileia (see n. 11); Egbert, Bishop of Bamberg (see n. 13). Sisters of Otto were Agnes (+1201), wife of King Philip II of France; Gertrude (+1213), wife of King Andrew II of Hungary; St. Hedwig (+1243), wife of Henry, Duke of Silesia-Breslau. Otto took the Cross in 1215 and returned ca. January 1218.

[8] Eustorgius of Montagu, Archbishop of Nicosia, 1217–50. He is referred to as a vicar of the Patriarch of Jerusalem in a letter concerning the crusade written to Thibaud, Count of Champagne, and to other French barons. Eustorgius was the brother of Guérin de Montagu, Master of the Hospitallers (see p. 93, n. 1), and Peter, Master of the Templars.

[9] Peter, Bishop of Raab (in Hungary), Suffragan of the primatial see of Strigonium, 1206–18.

[10] Thomas, Bishop of Erlau (in Hungary), 1217–24.

[11] Berthold V of Meran, Archbishop of Kalocza and Bacs (in Hungary), 1206–18, transferred to Aquileia as Patriarch, 1218–51. He was brother of Duke Otto of Meran (see n. 7) and of Bishop Egbert of Bamberg.

[12] Robert of Ableiges, Bishop of Bayeux, 1206–31.

[13] Egbert of Meran, Bishop of Bamberg, 1203–37, another brother of Otto of Meran.

[14] Engelbert, Bishop of Zeitz (formerly Naumburg), in the Archdiocese of Magdeburg, 1207–42.

[15] Otto of Aldenburg, Bishop of Münster, 1204–18.

[16] Otto VI, Bishop of Utrecht, 1215–28.

[17] Walter of Avesnes (in Flanders) left home in 1217, but had already returned by the spring of 1218. His family contributed several members to the crusades, among whom Jacques of Avesnes had been conspicuous on the Third Crusade.

CHAPTER 2

The Patriarch of Jerusalem,[1] with great humility on the part of the clergy and the people, reverently lifted up the wood of the life-giving Cross, and set out from Acre on the sixth day after the feast of All Saints [Nov. 6, 1217], into the camp of the Lord which had moved to Recordane.[2] Now this sweet wood had been preserved up to this time, even after the loss of the Holy Land. When the conflict of the Saracens with the Christians was threatening in the time of Saladin, as we have learned from our ancestors, the Cross was cut in pieces; part was carried into battle and was lost there,[3] and part was preserved, which now is displayed. With such a standard, we advanced in orderly array, through the plain of Faba[4] as far as the fountain of Tubania,[5] toiling much on that day; and when we had sent scouts ahead, seeing the dust that was being stirred up by our enemies, we were uncertain whether they were hastening to attack us or to flee. On the following day we set out through the mountains of Gilboa,[6] which were on our right, with a swamp on the left, to Bethsan[7] where the enemy had pitched camp; but fearing the arrival of the army of the living God, that was so numerous, and that was proceeding in so orderly a way, they broke camp and fled, leaving the land to be devastated by the soldiers of Christ. Thence, crossing the Jordan on the vigil of Saint Martin [Nov. 11], we washed our bodies at leisure in it, and we rested throughout two days in the same place, finding an abundance of food and fodder; then on the shore of the Sea of Galilee we made three days' rest, wandering through places in which Our Savior deigned to work miracles, and conversed with men in His

[1] Ralph of Merencourt, former Bishop of Sidon, Patriarch of Jerusalem, 1214–25.

[2] South of Acre; today known as Chirbet Kurdâne.

[3] At the battle of Hattin (July 4, 1187), when Saladin destroyed the army of the kingdom of Jerusalem.

[4] Al-Fula, directly southeast of Nazareth.

[5] West of Nazareth and known today as Ain Tubaûn.

[6] A mountainous region and city, east of the Jordan. The mountain is known today as Jebel Osha.

[7] Southwest of the Sea of Tiberias; Bethsan, or Beisan, the ancient Scythopolis.

corporal presence. We looked upon Bethsaida,[8] the city of Andrew and Peter, then reduced to a small casale; places were pointed out to us where Christ called His disciples, walked on the sea with dry feet, fed the multitudes in the desert, went up into the mountain alone to pray, and the place where He ate with His disciples after the resurrection; and thus we returned to Acre, carrying our sick and our needy brethren through Capharnaum [9] on beasts of burden.

CHAPTER 3

In the second raid we approached the foot of Mount Tabor, finding first a lack of water, but afterwards plenty when we dug for it. Our leaders despaired of the ascent of the mountain until, after a Saracen boy had told them that the camp could be seized, they formed a plan. Indeed, on the first Sunday of the Advent of the Lord [Dec. 3], when the gospel was read—"Go into the town that is over against you" [1]—the Patriarch went forward with the sign of the Cross, with bishops and clergy, up the ascent of the mountain, praying and singing psalms. Although the mountain was steep on all sides and high, and apparently impossible to ascend beyond the well-trodden footpath, nevertheless the knights and their attendants, horsemen and foot soldiers, ascended manfully. John, King of Jerusalem, with the army of the Lord, overthrew the chatelain and the emir together in the first attack; he reduced to flight and terror the defenders of the fort, who, to defend the mountain, fearlessly resisted the enemy outside the gates. But the King then lost as much in merit by descending as he had gained by ascending; for in descending on the same Sunday and making others descend, he gave courage to the infidel by the space of time that was granted to them; but we do not know by what judgment of God or by what plan of the leaders the army of the Lord descended then and withdrew ingloriously; this, however, we do know, that the eye of

---

[8] A ruined town on the northeast side of the Lake of Galilee, at the mouth of the Jordan. Probably the present et-Tell.

[9] A ruined city on the western shore of the Sea of Galilee, probably the present Tell Hum.

[1] Matthew 21:2.

the human mind cannot penetrate the abysses of divine decrees. Now many Templars and Hospitallers and certain seculars were wounded in the second ascent of the mountain when they had received forces from the camp, but few died. We believe that Christ Our Lord reserved this triumph of the mountain for Himself alone, since He ascended it with a few disciples, pointing out there the glory of the future resurrection. Furthermore, in the first and second raids, the Christians carried off with them a very great multitude of captives, men and women, and even children. Now the Bishop of Acre [2] baptized the little ones, whom he could win over by a gift or by a prayer, and apportioning them among religious women, he arranged for them to receive instruction.

CHAPTER 4

On the third raid,[1] in which the Patriarch, with the sign of the Cross, and the holy pontiffs took no part, we sustained many losses and hardships, as much through highwaymen, as by the severity of the winter, especially on our journey on the vigil of the Nativity of the Lord [Dec. 24], when many poor men and beasts perished from cold, and on the holy night itself, when we endured a severe storm on land, produced by wind and rain in the country of Tyre and Sidon near Sarepta.

[2] Jacques de Vitry, a famous historian of the crusades, Bishop of Acre, Cardinal-Bishop of Tusculum, born *ca.* 1160, died 1240. He preached a crusade against the Albigensians 1210–13, and was on the expedition against Damietta, 1218–20. Shortly before his death he refused the Patriarchate of Jerusalem. His chief historical work for the crusades is found in his letters to Pope Honorius, and especially in his *Historia Orientalis seu Hierosolymitana*, which gives an eye-witness account of the Holy Land in the 13th century. This includes a geographical description of the country and a description of the magnetic compass. What is called Book III of this work is really part of the present work of Oliver.

[1] This expedition went towards Beaufort (Sakif Arnûn), a twin fortress to Toron, and situated at the other side of Nahr Litani.

CHAPTER 5

After this, the army of the Lord was divided into four parts. The King of Hungary and the King of Cyprus set out for Tripoli, where the youthful King of Cyprus ended his days.[1] After a short delay, the King of Hungary withdrew, to the great detriment of the Holy Land;[2] he took away with him pilgrims also, and helmets, horses, and beasts of burden, with weapons, although he was repeatedly warned by the Patriarch that he should not retreat thus; finally, being excommunicated, he departed stubbornly with his retinue. Another division of lazy and cowardly pilgrims who, lying down, consumed the abundance of temporal things, remained in Acre. But the King of Jerusalem and the Duke of Austria, with the Hospitallers of Saint John[3] and the bishops mentioned above, and certain others, in a short time manfully and faithfully strengthened the fort in Caesarea of Palestine, although the arrival of the enemy was frequently announced. Through this fort, God granting, the city itself will be restored. In the basilica of the Prince of the Apostles, the Patriarch with six bishops solemnly celebrated the feast of the Purification [Feb. 2, 1218]. Moreover the Templars[4] with Lord Walter of Avesnes and some pilgrim helpers, and the

---

[1] Hugh I, a Lusignan (*see* p. 12, n. 5), died on January 10, 1218, at the age of twenty-three.

[2] Andrew had become sick during the early part of the crusade, and had gone to Acre. He was present in Tripoli at the marriage of Bohemond IV with Melisende, sister of Hugh I. Not long afterwards (early in 1218), he returned to Europe by way of Anatolia.

[3] The Knights Hospitallers of St. John of Jerusalem, a powerful and wealthy military order. They began in 1092 with the building of a hospital for pilgrims, and followed a rule based on that of St. Augustine. From 1309 to 1523 they were known as the Knights of Rhodes, and from 1530 to 1798 as the Knights of Malta. It is still a religious and secular order in the Catholic church, and there are both Anglican and Lutheran branches, the famous St. John's Ambulance Corps, which did such fine work in England during the recent war, being a subsidiary.

[4] The Knights of the Temple, founded in 1118 for the defense of the Christian kingdom of Jerusalem, got their name from their headquarters near the Temple in Jerusalem. They followed a rule especially written for them by St. Bernard. They became the most powerful of the military orders, and were immensely wealthy. To please King Philip the Fair, Pope Clement V suppressed them in 1312.

Hospitallers from the House of the Teutons,[5] began to refortify the Pilgrims' Castle,[6] which was formerly called Destroit. This is located in the diocese of Caesarea between Caiphas and Caesarea. Its location is as follows:

CHAPTER 6

A large and lofty promontory overhangs the sea, naturally fortified by cliffs to the north, the west, and the south; toward the east is a strong tower erected some time ago by the Templars, and held as well in war as in time of truce. Now the tower was placed there originally because of bandits who threatened strangers ascending to Jerusalem along the narrow path, and descending from it; it was not far from the sea, and on account of the narrow path it was called Destroit. When the fort of Caesarea was built and completed, the Templars, digging constantly crosswise through the promontory, and laboring for six weeks, finally came upon the first foundation, where the ancient wall appeared thick and long. Money also was found there in a coinage unknown to modern times, which was conferred by the goodness of the Son of God on His soldiers to alleviate their expenses and labors. Next, while they were digging and carrying out sand in an anterior section, another shorter wall was found, and between the flat surface of the walls fountains of fresh water freely gushed forth; the Lord also supplied an abundance of stones and cement. Two towers were built at the front of the fort of hewn and fitted stones of such greatness that

[5] The Teutonic Knights were a military order which had its beginning in a tent-hospital for Germans during the siege of Acre in 1189. Its members were German priests, knights, and serving brothers. In the 13th century they conquered and took possession of pagan Prussia, but declined after 1400 from defeats inflicted by the Poles. They turned Lutheran in the 16th century, were secularized in 1805, and were reorganized in Austria in 1834 as a Catholic order to care for the sick. The order now contains professed knights, priests, and sisters. In addition, it exists as a noble order of honor.

[6] Athlit, along the coast of Palestine, was fortified at the same time as Caesarea. It is southeast of the edge of Mount Carmel. The Franks had occupied it in the 11th century, and built the tower of Destroit on the last spur of Mount Carmel. Walter of Avesnes called himself its godfather, and referred to the fort as Château-Pélerin.

one stone is with difficulty drawn in a cart by two oxen. Both towers are one hundred feet in length and seventy-four in width. Their thickness encloses two sheds to protect soldiers. Their height rising up much exceeds the height of the promontory. Between the two towers a new and high wall was completed with ramparts; and by a wonderful artifice, armed horsemen can go up and down within. Likewise another wall slightly distant from the towers extends from one side of the sea to the other, having a spring of living water enclosed. The promontory is encircled on both sides by a high new wall, as far as the rocks. The fort contains an oratory with a palace and several houses. The primary advantage of this building is that the assembly of Templars, having been led out of Acre, a sinful city and one filled with all uncleanness, will remain in the garrison of this fort up until the restoration of the walls of Jerusalem. The territory of this fortress abounds in fisheries, salt mines, woods, pastures, fields, and grass; it charms its inhabitants with vines that have been or are to be planted, by gardens and orchards. Between Acre and Jerusalem there is no fortification which the Saracens hold, and therefore the unbelievers are harmed greatly by that new fortress; and with the fear of God pursuing them, they are forced to abandon these cultivated regions. This structure has a naturally good harbor which will be better when aided by artifice; it is six miles away from Mount Tabor. The construction of this castle is presumed to have been the cause of the destruction of the other, because in the long wide plain, which lies between the mountainous districts of this camp and of Mount Tabor, no one could safely plough or sow or reap because of fear of those who lived in it.

CHAPTER 7

The Bishop of Münster [1] fell asleep in the Lord at Caesarea. Master Thomas,[2] a theologian and a good and clear-minded doctor, brought to an end his last day at the Castle of the Son of God.[3]

[1] Bishop Otto (*see* p. 13, n. 15) died on March 6, 1218, at Caesarea.
[2] Nothing further is known of him.
[3] The Castle of the Son of God was the same as the Château-Pélerin.

CHAPTER 8

After this the army of the Lord returned to Acre. The bishops of Germany and many others prepared themselves to cross the sea after having delayed a short time in the Land of Promise. There was expected a second new passage, and especially a fleet coming from the north,[1] which it was hoped would sail through the narrow sea of Carthage. From the beginning of the preaching of the Cross of Christ, the province of Cologne, with great zeal and also at enormous expense, prepared almost three hundred ships, some of which survived, but others perished from the force of a storm; but a large part arrived at Acre with great courage on the part of the warriors. Discord arose there when certain ones wished to proceed, and others desired to spend the winter in the siege of that most powerful fort which is called Alcatia.[2] And there the fleet was divided: part spent the winter at Gaeta and Corneto; the other part besieged Alcatia under two leaders, Count William of Holland[3] and Count George of Wied.[4] This fort [Alcatia] was captured by the Germans and the Frisians. Until that time they had carried on the siege against a great multitude of Saracens whom the Templars and the Knights of Saint James[5] fought manfully, to-

---

[1] This journey is described in *De Itinere Frisonum* taken from Emo's *Chronicon*, and edited by Röhricht in *Quinti Belli Sacri Scriptores Minores*, pp. 59–70. Three hundred ships were prepared at Cologne. Some remained, others perished, but the majority came to Lisbon in Portugal. The fleet left by the Lauwerzee on May 31, 1216, and arrived at Acre on April 26, 1218. (Röhricht, *Beiträge*, II, 239 ff., gives more details, with the chief sources.)

[2] Alcacer de Sol, on the Rio Sado, west of Setubal in Portugal.

[3] William I, Count of Holland, 1204–36, of the house of Petersheim, was under excommunication when he took the Cross. He led the Frisians in Spain, and fought very bravely against the Mohammedans. On September 15, 1219, he prepared to depart from the crusade. By April 19, 1220, he was with Frederick II.

[4] Count George of Wied was the leader of the Frisian fleet against Spain and Egypt. He was a brother of Dietrich, Archbishop of Trier, 1212–42, and coleader (with Count William of Holland) of the fleet that sailed from the Lauwerzee.

[5] Oliver uses the term "Spatarians" for the Knights of the Military Order of St. James of the Sword (de la Spatha), founded in Spain about the year 1158. Their chief purpose was to aid Christianity by war upon the Saracens. Their distinguishing badge was a red sword on a white cloak.

gether with the army of the Queen of Portugal.[6] Finally the Saracens were conquered by divine strength; one of their kings was killed, and with him a great many were massacred or led into captivity.[7]

CHAPTER 9

The province of Cologne was stirred up to the service of the Savior of the world through signs which appeared in heaven. For in the province of Cologne and in the diocese of Münster in a village of Fresia, namely, Bedum, in the month of May on the sixth day before Pentecost [May 16], when the Cross was preached there, a triple form appeared in the heavens, one white toward the north, another toward the south of the same color and shape, a third in the middle, tinted with color, having the fork of a cross, and the figure of a man suspended upon it, with arms raised and extended, with the mark of nails in hands and feet, and with bowed head. This middle one was between two others on which there was no likeness of a human body. At another time and in another place, in a village of Fresia, at the time of the preaching of the Cross, there appeared alongside of the sun a cross of a blue color; more saw this than saw the former. The third apparition was in the diocese of Utrecht in the village of Dokkum where Saint Boniface was martyred. When on the feast of the same martyr [June 5] many thousands had assembled there for the station of the same martyr, there appeared a large white cross as if one beam had been artificially placed over another. This sign we all saw. Now it moved gradually from the north to the south. But we believe that the two apparitions were manifested so that all the ambiguity of the first vision might be removed, as the Apostle says about the resurrection

[6] The King of Portugal, 1211–23, was Alfonso II. His wife, whom he married in 1207 or 1208, was Urraca, daughter of Alfonso III, King of Castile.

[7] The *Gesta Crucigerorum Rhenanorum* (*Quinti Belli Sacri Scriptores Minores*, ed. Röhricht, pp. 27–56) and the *De Itinere Frisonum* (*ibid.*, pp. 57–70) give few details about this capture of Alcacer (known to the Arabs as Kafr Abû Danes under the rule of Abd Allah ibn Muhammed ibn Wazir. —Röhricht, *Beiträge*, II, 241–42, gives full details).

of Christ, "that He appeared to Cephas, afterwards to the eleven apostles, and next to more than five hundred brethren."[1]

CHAPTER 10

In the year of grace 1218, in the month of March, ships [1] began to sail to the port of Acre from the province of Cologne with other small ships from the province of Bremen and Trier. Thus was accomplished that plan formed in the Lateran Council at Rome under the Lord Pope Innocent of good memory, for leading the army of the Christians into the land of Egypt. Therefore in the month of May, after the Ascension of the Lord [May 24], when the ships had been prepared, and the galleys had been equipped with arms, and the other ships had been loaded, there set out from Acre, John, King of Jerusalem; the Patriarch with the bishops of Nicosia, Bethlehem,[2] and Acre; the Duke of Austria with the three Houses,[3] and a copious multitude of Christians. The fleet was ordered to assemble at the Castle of the Son of God, which is called the Castle of the Pilgrims; then with a north wind blowing, when the King, the Duke, and the masters of the Houses came to the appointed place, the host of the Lord set out under full sail, arriving at the harbor of Damietta on the third day. Now the above-mentioned leaders, since they had made a slight delay at the castle, could not follow after the host until the sixth day after their departure from the harbor of Acre. Many also who had not been prepared and who made some delay at Acre, after those who sailed first, either remained there entirely or were driven back into Acre by the violence of the winds; or, being tossed about for three or four weeks, were delayed on the sea. The Archbishop of Rheims [4] and the Bishop of Limoges [5] remained in Acre because of their advanced

[1] I Corinthians 15:5-6.

[1] The Latin word *cogones* has here been freely translated "ships."
[2] The Patriarch Ralph, the bishops of Nicosia and Acre, and the Duke of Austria have been identified above. The Bishop of Bethlehem was Regnier, *ca.* 1207-27.
[3] The Templars, Hospitallers, and Teutonic Knights.
[4] Alberic, Archbishop of Rheims since 1207, who died on December 24, 1218.
[5] John de Veirac, Bishop of Limoges, 1197(98)-1218.

THE CAPTURE OF DAMIETTA

years. The Bishop of Limoges died there; the Archbishop of Rheims, having returned on the passage of the Holy Cross, perished on the way.

Now upon coming to land at the port of Damietta, they chose the Count of Saarbrücken [6] as their leader, and captured the hostile land on the third day [May 29] without any loss of blood, before the King and the aforesaid dukes followed them. For when a few Saracens advanced upon the knights at the harbor, a certain Frisian, with his right knee planted on the ground, turned his shield with his left hand, and brandished and hurled an iron spear with the right. A Saracen horseman watched him, thinking he was playing, when suddenly horse and rider, struck down by the Frisian, perished and fell to the ground. When the others fled, abandoning their baggage, the Christians fixed the boundaries of the camp between the seashore and the bank of the river Nile, to the great admiration of those following when they saw the tents that had been set up. God brought about this wonderful fact, that upon their first arrival the water of the river, though it was joined to the sea and on many occasions afterwards was of a salty taste, was drawn up fresh all the way to the casale which is almost a mile above Damietta. A short time after the arrival of the Christians there took place an almost complete eclipse of the moon; and although it usually comes from natural causes at the time of full moon, yet because Our Savior says, "There shall be signs in the sun and moon," [7] we interpreted this eclipse to the disfavor of the Saracens, as if it portended the failure of the very ones who impute the moon to themselves, putting great strength in the waning or waxing moon. Now it is read in Quintus Curtius [8] that when Alexander the Macedonian, the hammer of the whole world, set out against Darius and Porus from Greece into Asia, and his well-ordered battle lines proceeded on this side and that, there occurred an eclipse of the moon. Alexander, interpreting this in favor of the Greeks against the Medes and the Persians, encouraged his men, fought against Darius, and conquered him.

---

[6] Simon II, Count of Saarbrücken, 1211–33.
[7] Luke 21:25.
[8] *Historiae Alexandri Magni*, IV, 40. This is the only reference made to the name of a classical writer throughout the present work.

CHAPTER 11

A tower located in the middle of the river had to be captured before crossing. The Frisians, however, who were impatient of delay, crossed the Nile and carried off the animals of the Saracens. Wishing to pitch camp on the farther shore, they held their ground, fighting against the Saracens who came out of their city to oppose them. They were recalled through obedience because it did not seem wise to our leaders that a tower filled with pagans should be left behind the Christians. Meanwhile the Duke of Austria and the Hospitallers of Saint John prepared two ladders on two ships, and the Teutons and Frisians fortified a third ship with bulwarks, setting up a small fortress on the top of the mast without hanging a ladder. Their head, their leader, and their counselor was Count Adolph of Berg,[1] a noble and powerful man, the brother of the Archbishop of Cologne.[2] The Count died at Damietta before the tower was captured. The ladders of the Duke and of the Hospitallers were directed against the tower about the time of the feast of Saint John the Baptist [June 24], with the Saracens defending it manfully. The ladder of the Hospitallers was shattered and crashed with the mast, hurling its warriors headlong; the ladder of the Duke, being broken in like manner at almost the same time, sent up to heaven soldiers who were vigorous and well armed, wounded in body to the advantage of their souls, crowned with a glorious martyrdom. The overjoyed Egyptians, mocking us violently, raised their voices, beating drums and sounding sackbuts;[3] gloom and sadness invaded the Christians. But the ship of the Germans and Frisians cast anchor between the tower and the city, causing great losses to the Egyptians through its ballistae,[4] which had been set up within, especially to those who were standing on the bridge that extended between the city and the tower. The ship

---

[1] Count Adolph V, 1189–1218. He died before Damietta on August 7, 1218.

[2] St. Engelbert II, just made archbishop earlier in the year 1218. He died in 1225.

[3] An obsolete musical instrument, a bass trumpet with a slide like that of a trombone for altering the pitch.

[4] An ancient military engine resembling a bow, stretched with cords and thongs, used to hurl stones or other missiles.

itself, however, was being quite violently attacked by the warriors of the city, by the javelins of the tower and of the bridge, and by Greek fire. Finally it was seized upon by the fire; and although the Christians feared that it would be entirely destroyed, its defenders bravely extinguished the flames. Likewise pierced by arrows within and without, both in that fortress placed on the top of the mast and even on the ropes of the rigging, the ship, bearing the great honor of Christianity, was brought back to its position. No slight damage was dealt out and endured by one ship of the Templars, fortified by bulwarks which were held alongside of the tower at the time of this assault.

CHAPTER 12

However, we realized that the tower could neither be captured by the blows of petraries [1] or of trebuchets [2] (for this was attempted for many days); nor by bringing the fort closer, because of the depth of the river; nor by starvation, because of the surroundings of the city; nor by undermining, because of the roughness of the water flowing about. With the Lord showing us how and providing an architect,[3] and with the Germans and the Frisians providing supplies and labor, we joined two ships which we bound together sturdily by means of beams and ropes and so prevented (by their closely connected structure) the danger of drifting. We erected four masts and the same number of sailyards, setting up on the summit a strong fortress joined with poles and a network fortification. We covered it with skins about its circumference, as a protection from the attacks of their machine, and over its top as a defense against the Greek fire. Under the fortress was made a ladder, hung by very strong ropes and stretching out thirty cubits beyond the prow. This task having been successfully completed in a short time, the leaders of the army were invited to see it, so that if anything was lacking that ought to be supplied by material or by human ingenuity, they would point it out. They replied that such a work of wood had never before been wrought

[1] A military engine of the medieval period for hurling stones.
[2] This also was a medieval military engine for casting heavy missiles.
[3] Oliver himself, as we learn from Jacques de Vitry, II, 292.

upon the sea. We realized that we must hasten, because, by frequent blows of the machines, the bridge which conveyed the enemies of the faith from the city to the tower in great part had been destroyed. Therefore on the sixth day before the feast of Saint Bartholomew [Aug. 18], we made a procession barefoot to the Holy Cross with devotion on the part of our people. After humbly imploring divine assistance that the affair might be free from all envy and empty boasting, we summoned to the execution of this task some men of every nation that was then in the army, although the nation of Germans and Frisians would suffice to fill and direct the ships.

CHAPTER 13

On the feast of Saint Bartholomew [Aug. 24], the sixth day, since the Nile had violently overflowed and the force of the waters greatly hindered our work, with the greatest difficulty and danger this engine was dragged against the torrent from the place in which it had been made, to the tower. A smaller ship, a companion of this machine, went along spreading its sails. The clergy, barefoot, walked as suppliants on the shore. When they had come to the tower, that twofold arrangement could not be turned around toward the west side, but by moving up it was placed directly toward the northern section. The ropes and anchors were finally made firm, although the force of the flooding waters strove to drive it back. Six or more machines were drawn up on the top of the towers of the city, and were placed there to shatter it. Now one, more dangerous than the others, being destroyed after a few blows, ceased its action; but the others without any intermission cast out stones like hail. And no less a danger did the first ship withstand, located at the foot of the tower. The Greek fire from the tower of the river close at hand came from the city afar like lightning and was able to inspire fear; but by sour liquid and gravel, and other means of extinguishing it, those who were toiling were aided.

The Patriarch lay prostrate in the dust before the wood of the Cross; the clergy, standing barefoot, garbed in liturgical robes, cried out to heaven. The defenders of the tower with lances extended, smeared the front of the ladder with oil; next they added fire which caused it to burst into flames. And when the Christians who were on it ran to put out the fire, they pressed on the head of the ladder with their weight so much that the movable bridge placed near its edge was made to bend. The standard bearer of the Duke of Austria fell from the ladder, and the Saracens captured the banner of the Duke. The Babylonians,[1] thinking that they were victorious, shouted madly, disturbing the air with their clamor. The Christians, descending from their horses, threw themselves down in supplication, beating their hands; their faces streamed with tears of sorrow as they protested the pity they had for those who were enduring peril in the depth of the river, and the loss of all Christendom. In answer to this devotion of the people and the raising of their hands to heaven, divine kindness lifted the ladder, the tears of the faithful extinguished the fire; and thus our men, with renewed vigor, manfully fought with the defenders of the tower by means of swords, pikes, clubs, and other weapons. A certain young knight of the diocese of Liège was the first to ascend the tower; a certain young Frisian, holding a flail by which grain is usually threshed, but which was prepared for fighting by an interweaving with chains, lashed out bravely to the right and to the left, knocked down a certain man holding the saffron standard of the Sultan and took the banner away from him. One came after another, vanquishing the enemy, who were known to be hard and cruel in their resistance. O ineffable kindness of God! O unexplainable joy of Christians! After lamentation and grief, after weeping and groaning, we saw joy and triumph. "We praise Thee, O God," [2] "Blessed be the Lord God of Israel," [3] and other canticles of thanksgiving to the heavens we sang for joy, our voices being mingled with tears and our praises repeated.

[1] The Mohammedans of Egypt were often referred to as Babylonians, because Cairo was usually referred to as Babylon, owing to its closeness to the ancient city of that name in Egypt.

[2] A hymn sung in the office of Matins after the 9th lesson, and as a prayer of thanksgiving at times of great rejoicing. It is called the Ambrosian Hymn, but the author is unknown.

[3] The canticle of Zachary (Luke 1: 68–79), said daily at Lauds.

CHAPTER 14

Meanwhile the Saracens, who had withdrawn to the inner part of the tower, having put fire under the top part of the tower, burned it; our men, though victorious, retreated over the ladder, not being able to stand the heat. But the bridge, which had been prepared in the lower part of the fortification, was let down to the narrow foot of the tower, with deep waters surging about on all sides. With iron hammers the victors attacked the door while the Saracens who were within defended it. Both fortifications remained impregnable; the rungs of the ladder, in part, and the circuit of the work which was held together by very strong ropes were pierced by blows of the machines. From the ninth hour of the sixth day until the tenth hour of the following Saturday [Aug. 25] this danger lasted. But the net-like arrangement which protected the ladder remained unharmed, along with the fort in which were stationed the ballistae and the petraries, which protected them. Finally, being enclosed in the tower, the Saracens sought a conference, and, under a guarantee that their lives would be spared, they surrendered to the Duke of Austria, except those who on the preceding night had thrown themselves headlong through the windows and escaped the narrow bounds of the tower; several of them were drowned in the river and perished. But the captives numbered one hundred men.

CHAPTER 15

Although from that day the Babylonians were confused and terrified, and, as it was thought, prepared for flight, our leaders fell into idleness and laziness according to their custom. They invented a motive for deferring negotiations, and they did not imitate Judas Macchabeus who "seeing that the time served him" [1] gave no rest to the enemy.

---

[1] I Macchabees 12:1.

CHAPTER 16

The ships prepared to withdraw. A great multitude of Frisians and Teutons set out in the next passage of the Holy Cross. In that passage [1] came certain Romans, and after that the Bishop of Albano, the Delegate of the Apostolic See,[2] and with him a Roman prince;[3] next the Archbishop of Bordeaux [4] who made a useful delay; the bishops of Angers,[5] Mantua,[6] Humana,[7] and Salpi;[8] next Master Robert of Courçon, Cardinal-Bishop of the title of Saint Stephen on Monte Celio;[9] the bishops of Paris,[10] Gerona,[11] Erlau,[12] and Hungary, who died before the crossing of the river on the sand of Damietta, and Cardinal Robert likewise. The Count of Nevers [13] came also, who, when danger threatened, retreated, to the scandal of the Christians. The Count of La Marche,[14] and the Count of

---

[1] August and September 1218.

[2] Pelagius Galvani, a Spaniard or Portuguese by birth. Cardinal-Bishop of Albano, 1211–40. He has been blamed by many for the ultimate failure of the crusade. His unwillingness to accept terms considered favorable by the Christian lay leaders was due to his anxiety to capture Cairo itself. His high-handed methods alienated many of the lay lords. In the Church he had a distinguished career. Pope Innocent III made him Cardinal-Deacon of the Title of S. Lucia, then Cardinal-Priest in 1206. He was Papal Legate on the crusade, as Oliver mentions. After its disastrous ending he returned to Europe and was employed by Pope Honorius III on many occasions. He died in Monte Cassino, January 27, 1240.

[3] According to Hoogeweg (p. 187, n. 2), this was James, Count of Andria. Perhaps he was a relative of Hugh I, Duke of Andria, ca. 1173–1240.

[4] William II, Amanieu de Geniès, 1207–27.

[5] William of Beaumont, Bishop of Angers, 1202–40. He became Archbishop in 1207.

[6] Henry, Bishop of Mantua, 1193–1220(25?).

[7] Gerard III, first mentioned in 1204, and who was dead by 1228.

[8] Unknown.

[9] Chancellor of the University of Paris, and Cardinal, 1212–19. He was a brother of Walter of Nemours, Chamberlain of France. The two brothers departed for the crusade in 1218.

[10] Peter of Nemours, Archbishop of Paris, 1208–19.

[11] Raymond of Palafolls, Archbishop of Gerona, 1214–18.

[12] For the bishops of Erlau and Hungary, see p. 13, n. 10 and p. 13, n. 11. Thomas of Hungary did not die as is stated here, but returned home in September 1218.

[13] See p. 30, n. 18.

[14] Hugh II of Angoulême of La Marche, 1208–49.

Bar [15] and his son,[16] Brother William of Chartres, Master of the army of the Temple,[17] Hervé of Vierzon,[18] Ithier of Toucy,[19] Oliver, son of the King of England,[20] and many others of the knightly order, and common people, ended their days at Damietta. Many martyrs for Christ, more confessors of Christ, being delivered from human cares at Damietta, went to the Lord.

CHAPTER 17

"He is wise in heart and mighty in strength Who doth great things and unsearchable things without number and marvelous. Who judges those that are high, Who places the humble on high." [1] He alone was magnified in the siege of Damietta. For not as in other expeditions against the Saracens, when various opportunities were arranged through human wisdom or the agency of the warriors, but through Himself did He work miraculously through the power of His divinity what man did not presume to seek; giving honor not to kings or other princes or nations, but to His Name, that the prophetic promise might be fulfilled in us sinners: "The Lord will fight for you and you will hold your peace." [2]

CHAPTER 18

After the tower had been captured that was located in the depths of the river Nile, Saphadin,[1] grown old with evil days and sickness,

[15] Milo III, Count of Bar-sur-Seine since 1189. He died on August 18, 1219 at the siege of Damietta. His two sons also were killed there.

[16] Walter of Puiset, son of Milo.

[17] William of Puiset, called William of Chartres, son of Milo and brother of Walter, Master of the Temple, 1209–19.

[18] Hervé IV of Donzy, Count of Nevers since 1199, by his marriage to Mahaut, daughter of Peter of Courtenay and his wife Agnes. He died on January 22, 1223.

[19] Perhaps a descendant of Ithier III, oldest son of Narjot I, Lord of Toucy, 1147–73. Ithier III had gone on the crusade with Louis VII.

[20] Oliver was an illegitimate son of John Lackland, King of England, 1199–1216.

---

[1] Job 9:4; 5:9; 5:11.
[2] Exodus 14:14.

[1] Malik-al-Adil Seif ed Din, brother of Saladin, died on August 31, 1218. Of his many sons, two deserve mention here: Malik-al-Kamil Mohammed, Sultan

the disinheritor of his cousins and the usurper of the kingdoms of Asia, died and was buried in hell. Afterwards on the feast of Saint Denis [Oct. 9] the Saracens, coming unexpectedly with armed galleys and invading the most important of the camps where the Romans had set up tents, were repulsed by a small band of Christians; King John of Jerusalem fought manfully there at the exhortation of the Bishop of Bethlehem, when he pursued them as they ran back quickly to their galleys; nevertheless, they were unable to escape the swords of their pursuers and the whirling of the river. Now, like the Egyptians formerly in the raging waters of the Red Sea, so in the Nile about one thousand were drowned, as we learned afterwards from the Saracens.

On the feast of Saint Demetrius [Oct. 26], who is said to have been the uterine brother of the blessed Denis, the enemy at dawn invaded the camp of the Templars, and though causing us a slight loss, they were driven away by our alert horsemen, to the bridge which they had built a short distance from us in the upper part of the river; they were killed to the number of five hundred, as we learned from deserters.

CHAPTER 19

Next, since many of the Christian people were pleasing to the Lord, it was necessary that temptation should prove them. Jonas, being cast out into the sea because of the trouble of the tempest, and being shut up in the belly of a fish, returned to dry land when he had been proved. The Apostle escaped when he had been tried by a threefold shipwreck; the people of the Lord deserved to be tried when they had practised a three days' fast, which the clergy observed obediently on bread and water, and when many processions had been ordered by the venerable Lord Pelagius, the Bishop of Albano, Legate of the Apostolic See. For on the vigil of Saint Andrew the Apostle [Nov. 29], in the middle of the night, the

---

of Egypt; and Malik-al-Moadden Isa, known to the Christians as Coradin, Lord of Damascus.(*See* p. 36, n. 1.) At one time Richard the Lion-Hearted had proposed that Saphadin marry his sister, the widowed Queen of Sicily. Saphadin had united the empire of Saladin at the expense of Saladin's own sons, whom he dispossessed of their heritage. (*See* p. 52, n. 4–5.)

waves of the sea rose, swelling and making a terrible advance even to the camp of the faithful; the river, rushing in from the other direction, took us unaware. The tents floated off, the food supply was destroyed, fishes of the river and of the sea, as though fearing nothing, piled into our sleeping quarters, and we caught them with our hands, delights nevertheless which we were willing to be without. And unless, by the plan of the Holy Ghost, preparations had been made beforehand [1] on the rampart which had been made for other uses, the sea joined with the river would have dragged off to the enemy the men with the animals, and the ships with the weapons and food supplies. This danger, however, four ships, upon which had been erected fortresses to capture the city, did not escape; in one attack, they, along with a fifth ship which was caught in their midst, were driven to the opposite shore by the force of the winds, and were burned before our eyes with Greek fire. The Lord spared the labors of the Frisians and the Germans by whom the tower had been captured. Laden ships which were standing in the port of the sea were lost when their ropes were suddenly broken. This storm lasted for three continuous days. When this had elapsed, the Lord "Who consoles His people in every tribulation, comforts in all our afflictions, commanded the wind and the sea to be still, making it cease from raging." [2]

CHAPTER 20

Besides, many of the army were struck down by a certain plague against which physicians could find no remedy in all their skill.[1] A sudden pain attacked the feet and legs, and at the same time corrupt flesh covered the gums and teeth, taking away the power of chewing; a horrible blackness darkened the shins, and so having

[1] In the middle of October or early November.
[2] See Matthew 8:26; II Corinthians 1:4; Jonas 1:15.

[1] This disease reminds us of the troubles suffered by Richard on his crusade. He had pains in the mouth and lips, apparently from Vincent's infection or trench mouth. See Ambroise, *The Crusade of Richard the Lion Heart*, tr. and ed. by M. J. Hubert and J. L. LaMonte (New York, 1941), 11. 405–08, p. 196. The sickness described by Oliver seems to have been even more acute and resembles the disease known in modern times as scurvy.

been afflicted with a long stretch of illness, very many went to the Lord with much suffering. Certain ones, surviving until spring, escaped, being delivered by the advantage of heat.

CHAPTER 21

After the aforesaid tempest, the ships were prepared to cross the river; these, going up at great risk between the city and the captured tower, were greatly retarded by Greek fire and javelins. Wherefore it happened that one ship of the Templars,[1] carried away by the violence of the current, was cast over near the side of the city toward the enemy, who for a long time assailed it with barbots[2] and grappling irons, hurling out Greek fire and stones from the towers above; and since they could not prevail on account of the bravery of the defenders, they eagerly climbed up the ship, and throwing themselves headlong into it, descended upon the Templars. When they had fought there for a long time, the ship at last was pierced (whether by the enemy or by our own men we do not know) and sought the depths, drowning Egyptians with Christians, so that the top of the mast scarcely appeared above the water. And as Samson "killed many more at his death than he had killed before in his life,"[3] so also those martyrs dragged into the abyss of the waters along with themselves more than they could have killed with swords. But the citizens of Damietta mourned their bloody victory for almost seven days. Thereupon, while repairing the bridge they left a narrow opening, so that our ships could not go up without danger. But the Germans and the Frisians, fired with the zeal of righteous indignation, having no help except from heaven, manfully attacked the bridge with the smaller ship by whose aid the tower had been captured, and which the Gauls called "Holy Mother." Less than ten men of the above-mentioned nation climbed the bridge in the face of all the hardihood of the Babylonians, with a great multitude of Christians looking on and highly praising this boldness. They broke it down; and thus, with

[1] This is a chronological error. The loss of this ship occurred in early November before the storm. See Hoogeweg, p. 194, n. 1.
[2] A small vessel having its deck protected by an arched covering of leather.
[3] Judges 16:30.

the four ships upon which the bridge had been founded, they returned in triumph, leaving a way free and open for the ships sailing upward.

CHAPTER 22

When all this had been so accomplished, the Saracens, while awaiting the danger which threatened them, fortified the bank opposite us by means of ramparts and a clay-like substance with high wooden defenses, setting up machines and petraries there, taking from us the hope of crossing through that place. But from the casale, which is almost a mile away from the city, where this new fortification ended, all across the river they sank ships and fixed stakes in the eddies. Nevertheless the Legate of the Apostolic See, having the good desire of besieging the city, urged the ships gathered higher up to cross. Wherefore the ships, fortified by defenses and fortresses, and also by armed men with galleys and other ships, Christ being their leader, escaped the sunken ships mentioned above. But the enemy, pretending fear, placed three ranks of armed men opposite the position of our ships: one of foot soldiers above the bank with shields, which they call targes, ranged in lines; the second behind them like the first; the third of horsemen, long and terrible, violently harassing the position of the Christians with showers of stones and weapons.

In addition, on the night of the solemnity of Saint Agatha, virgin and martyr [Feb. 5, 1219], when the people of the faithful assembled who were to cross on the following day, rains and winds added much peril and difficulty to our men. But "God is faithful" and "will not permit you to be tempted beyond your strength," [1] and looking at the camp of His servants, He turned into ease and joy a thing which according to less important causes would have been difficult or impossible, renewing the wonders of His power. After the middle of the night He struck such terror to the Sultan of Babylon and his satraps that, abandoning the camp unknown even to the Egyptians whom he had ranged for resisting, they placed their hope in

[1] I Corinthians 10:13.

flight alone. A certain apostate who, having transgressed the law of the Christians for some time, had fought on the side of the Sultan, stood on the bank and cried out in French, "Why do you delay? Why are you afraid? Why do you hesitate? The Sultan has gone away." And having said this he asked to be taken back into a ship so that being put in their power he might give proof to his words. Therefore at early dawn, when the office of the Mass of the feast-day had been begun throughout the oratories of the Christians, these words, "Let us all rejoice in the Lord," [2] were announced to the Legate, the King, and the others. And so as the Egyptians fled, our men crossed eagerly and quickly with no hindrance from the enemy and no shedding of blood.

But the land of the enemy was so muddy and so difficult to land upon because of the rather deep waters that the horses, being driven without saddles or riders, could scarcely get up. The Templars, leaders in the ascent of the horses, having put up their banners, hurried to the city in a swift march, throwing down the wicked ones who came boldly from the gates to resist those who were advancing. "The axe shall not boast itself against him that cutteth with it nor shall the saw exalt itself against him by whom it is drawn." [3] To what shall we equal or compare this miracle except to that which is read concerning Benadab, King of Syria,[4] who besieged Samaria, reducing it greatly, to whom the Lord sent such terror that he fled abandoning his camp? And as the flight of the Syrians was announced to the Samaritans by the lepers who were at the entrance of the gate, so the flight of the Egyptians was announced by one who was a leper in his soul, that is to say, the aforesaid apostate; and as the people of the Samaritans gathered up the spoils left in the camp of the Syrians, so our army plundered the tents and booty of those who were fleeing; the victors seized many targes and all the galleys, along with the barbots and other ships, which were found below the casale as far as the city, with other spoils. Many warriors, having left their wives and children, fled

---

[2] These words begin the Introit on the Feast of St. Agatha and on many feasts of the Blessed Virgin.

[3] Isaias 10:15.

[4] *See* IV Kings 6:24; 7:3. The last reference applies to the following sentence.

from Damietta, terrified because of the unexpected crossing. And the city was besieged firmly in a circle, the army being joined together through the arrangement of a bridge touching both banks.

CHAPTER 23

However, through the idleness and laziness of those whose names God knows, it happened that as Coradin [1] arrived with the men of Aleppo and a great multitude, the enemy with renewed vigor and spirit seized that place [Mar. 3] from which our men had made a miraculous crossing; and thus, as we were besieging the city, they besieged us more dangerously; and unless by divine counsel the first camp which was between the sea and the river had been held by the Germans and Frisians especially, the port would have been taken from us and the whole business, greatly imperiled, would have wavered. But in order that the miracle of the crossing might become more famous, and be unhesitatingly ascribed to Christ alone, the Saracens reached such a point of temerity that at daybreak of the Saturday before "Oculi mei semper" Sunday [Mar. 9],[2] since we did not foresee such a danger, they drew nearer with a great multitude and pressed on as far as the rampart; but by divine assistance they were driven back, with a loss of horsemen and foot soldiers.

CHAPTER 24

In the year of grace 1219, Jerusalem, the queen of cities, which seemed impregnably fortified, was destroyed within and without by Coradin, son of Saphadin [Mar. 19 or 25].[1] Its walls and towers

[1] Al-Malik al Moadden Isa of Damascus, 1218–27. He assisted his father and brother in their wars with the Christians, both by bringing aid from Syria to Egypt, and by keeping up diversionary attacks on Christian positions in Syria.
[2] The third Sunday of Lent. The Introit of the Mass for this day begins with the words "Oculi mei."

[1] Jerusalem had been in the hands of the Mohammedans since 1187, when it was surrendered to Saladin. After Coradin destroyed the walls in 1219, he destroyed two fortresses also, Toron and Safita. He did this because he thought that the Christians would retake the city.

were reduced to heaps of stones except for the temple of the Lord and the tower of David. The Saracens took counsel about destroying the glorious sepulchre, and they threatened this through letters which they sent across to the citizens of Damietta for their own consolation; but no one presumed to set his hand to this act of boldness because of reverence for the place. For as they had written in the Koran, the book of their law, they believe that Jesus Christ Our Lord was conceived and born of the Virgin Mary and they protest that He lived without sin as a prophet and more than a prophet; they firmly assert that He gave sight to the blind, cleansed lepers, and raised the dead; they do not deny the word and the spirit of God, and that He ascended alive into heaven. But they do deny His Passion and Death, and also that the divine nature is united to the human nature in Christ. They likewise deny the Trinity of Persons. Therefore they ought to be called heretics rather than Saracens, but the use of the false name prevails. Therefore, at the time of truce, when their wise men went up to Jerusalem, they asked that copies of the Gospels be shown to them. These they kissed and venerated because of the purity of the law which Christ taught, and especially because of the Gospel of Luke: "The Angel Gabriel was sent," [2] which the learned among them often repeat and recall to mind. But their law, which Mohammed, under the dictation of the devil, gave to the Saracens, and which was written in Arabic by the ministry of Sergius, a monk, an apostate, and a heretic, began from the sword, is upheld by the sword, and will be ended in the sword. Mohammed was unlearned, as he himself gives evidence in his Koran, and what the forenamed heretic dictated, he promulgated and ordered to be observed through threats. For he was dissolute and warlike, and therefore he laid down a law concerning uncleanness and vanity, which those who live carnally on the side of pleasure carefully observe. And as truth and purity fortify our law, so worldly and human fear and carnal pleasure guard their error most firmly.[3]

[2] Luke 1:26.
[3] Compare the picture given here by Oliver with R. S. Darbishere, "The Moslem Antagonist," *Moslem World*, XXVIII (1938), 258–71.

CHAPTER 25

On Palm Sunday of the forementioned year [Mar. 31], our enemies, having made many threats that they would destroy themselves or all of us in one day, collected a fearful and innumerable army of horsemen and foot soldiers and rushed upon us, invading our ramparts on all sides, especially the bridge of the Templars and the Duke of Austria, which he was eager to defend with the Germans. The enemy, with picked soldiers, leaped from their horses and fought savagely with the Christians. On this side and that many fell dead and wounded, and finally, climbing the bridge, they burned part of it. The Duke of Austria ordered his men that when the bridge had been abandoned they should give approach and entrance to those who were pressing on us; but they did not presume to enter because of our army, which had ranged its lines as an aid to those defending the fortifications. The women fearlessly brought water and stones, wine and bread to the warriors; the priests persisted in prayer, binding up and blessing the wounds of the injured. On that day, we were not given the opportunity of carrying palms other than crossbows, bows, and arrows, lances and swords and shields, so violently did they attack and harass us from sunrise to almost the tenth hour—they who had come to destroy us in the desire of freeing the city; at last they retreated wearily with great losses.

CHAPTER 26

The spring passage was not imminent. The Duke of Austria was going to withdraw, he who for a year and a half had fought faithfully for Christ, full of devotion, humility, obedience, and generosity. Besides all the other innumerable expenses which he had incurred in the dealings of war and in private alms, he is believed to have bestowed on the house of the Teutons six thousand marks of silver or more, to obtain land; and on the new fort of the Templars fifty marks of gold. To it also the Earl of Chester [1] gave fifty marks of silver for the strengthening of its walls and towers.

CHAPTER 27

On the first of May a great multitude of pilgrims began to withdraw, leaving us in the greatest danger. But our kind and merciful Father, our leader and comrade in arms, Jesus Christ, "the protector and defender of those who hope in Him, for Whom it is easy to save either by many or by few," [1] did not permit the unbelievers to rush in upon us until new and recent pilgrims arrived with abundant aid; a supply of provisions and horses sent over by divine power gladdened the assembly of the faithful. Therefore, on the feast of the Ascension of the Lord [May 16], when the number of the soldiers of Christ was renewed, the untrustworthy enemy, according to their custom, rushed upon us by land and by water. As they could not prevail, though they made many attempts, they challenged our men particularly near the camp, losing and inflicting losses. But on July 31 they brought forward all the power which they could muster, and after many assaults, finally crossed the ramparts against the army of the Temple. Violently bursting the barriers, they put our foot soldiers to flight, to such an extent that the whole army of the Christians was then endangered. The knights and soldiery of France tried three times to drive them farther back beyond the rampart, but were unable to do so. The Saracens, when our wooden fortifications had been shattered, ranged lines of horsemen and foot soldiers within our walls; their shouts arose as they mocked us; the whole multitude prepared its retinue. Fear welled up in the Christians, but the spirit which came upon Gideon animated the Templars. The Master of the Temple, with the Marshal and other brothers who were then present, made an attack through a narrow approach and manfully put

[1] Ranulf, Earl of Chester, had helped John Lackland in the civil war in England. On Ash Wednesday, 1215, he took the Cross, and in 1218 set out for the East. He landed soon after the capture of the chain tower (*see* pp. 26–8). He returned to England about August 1, 1220.

[1] Psalms 17:31; I Kings 14:6.

the unbelievers to flight. The House of the Teutons and the counts and other knights of different nations, seeing the army of the Temple placed in such danger, quickly brought aid through entrances opposite them; thus the foot soldiers of the Saracens threw away their shields and were killed, except those whose headlong flight had snatched them from their killers. Our foot soldiers went out after our horsemen. The enemy retreated a short distance, their armed ranks holding out here and there, until evening twilight put an end to the battle. The Saracens went away first. Bodies of massacred wretches lay strewn near our rampart in great numbers, except those who were wounded seriously or slightly, and were brought back to the camp. Thus on that day did God save those who hoped in Him through the courage of the Templars and of those who, having worked together with them, committed themselves to the conflict. A few of our men were killed or captured.

CHAPTER 28

Almost all the machines prepared against the city were burned in a many-sided sortie of the defenders of Damietta. The Pisans, the Genoese, and the Venetians [1] stoutly affirmed that they would attack the city by means of four ships upon which ladders hung; "but they were not of the race of those men by whom salvation was brought to Israel;" [2] for they wished to make a name for themselves, going forward with trumpets and reed pipes and many standards. The Legate of the Apostolic See supplied copious funds to them from the common store, the King and others produced ropes and anchors in abundance according as they needed them. And so, attacking the city, they killed and wounded many on the first day; and the more often they made an attack afterward, so much the more were the walls strengthened by wooden towers and palisades; the defenders resisted the oncomers even more vigorously and efficaciously, and thus the ladders, injured by fire and several times

---

[1] These inhabitants of northern Italian cities frequently sent along contingents with the crusaders in return for commercial advantages. Thus, they sided with Pelagius in insisting upon the capture of Damietta, a town that seemed promising for commerce. (*See* p. 46.)

[2] I Macchabees 5:62.

repaired, were forced to the bank, and the attempt was fruitless. And so it was truly understood that by divine power alone would Damietta be delivered into the hands of the Christians.

CHAPTER 29

But we, insensible and unmindful of the benefits and wonderful deeds of God, which He had done, "provoked the eyes of His divine majesty" [1] against us through the idleness of the leaders and the complaints of the followers. The foot soldiers reproached the cowardice of the horsemen, the horsemen made light of the risks of the foot soldiers when they went out against the Saracens. Therefore it happened that on the feast of the beheading of Saint John the Baptist [Aug. 29], with our common faults urging us on, although scarcely any were to be found who would remain in the custody of the camp, we led forth a naval and land army and proceeded to the camp of the Babylonians between the sea and the river, where fresh water could not be found to drink. But taking up their tents, they pretended flight; and when our men had advanced to a point where it was clear that our adversaries did not wish to meet us in open combat, our leaders began a long debate whether they should advance or retreat; the feeling among them was divided. Meanwhile the ranks were scattered except for a group of those whom obedience bound in military discipline. The knights of Cyprus,[2] who were on the right flanks, showed their timidity to the Saracens as they made an attack from the side. The Italian foot soldiers fled first, after them horsemen of various nations, and certain Hospitallers of Saint John, while the Legate of the Roman See, and the Patriarch, who was carrying the Cross, begged them earnestly to stand their ground, but in vain. The heat of the sun was intense, the foot soldiers were burdened with the weight of their arms. The difficulty of the way increased the heat,

[1] Isaias 3:8.
[2] The knights of Cyprus, as we are informed in Eracles (32, 10, pp. 339-40 in *Rec. Hist. Crois.*), were about a hundred in number, and were under the command of Walter, Lord of Caesarea as early as 1217, Constable of Cyprus from at least 1210 to as late as 1220. He was killed June 24, 1229 before Nicosia while fighting for John d'Ibelin against the partisans of Emperor Frederick.

and those who had brought wine with them drank it unmixed in the distress of their thirst because of the lack of water. With all these things happening at the same time, those who defended themselves as they stood their ground and turned their backs on those who fled first in their breathless course were wiped out, collapsing without wounds. But the King, with the Templars, and the House of the Teutons, and the Hospitallers of Saint John, and the counts of Holland, and of Wied, of Saarbrücken and Chester, with Walter of Berthout,[3] several counts of France and of Pisa, and other knights, sustained the attack of the pursuers. The King was almost burned with Greek fire; these men all served as a protection for those who were fleeing. As often as they showed their faces to the enemy, so often did the enemy flee, but as they gradually returned, these men had to sustain the blows and weapons of the enemy.

Captured in that defense of Christianity were the Bishop-elect of Beauvais [4] and his brother; [5] the Chamberlain of France and his son; [6] the Viscount of Belmont and brother of the Bishop of Angers; [7] John of Arcis, a noble and vigorous man; [8] Henry of Uelmen; [9] and many others who were massacred or taken into captivity. Thirty-three Templars were captured or killed with the Mar-

[3] Walter III of Berthout, a noble of Brabant and Lord of Mechlin 1180–1219 (1220?).

[4] The Bishop-elect of Beauvais was Milon of Chatillon-Neuilly, 1217–34, son of Gaucher, Lord of Chatillon-sur-Marne and of Helvis, Lady of Nanteuil. He left for the Orient on the news of the death of Alberic, Archbishop of Rheims, whose diocese he had been administering. He was not freed from the Saracens until 1222.

[5] André of Nanteuil who had been among the "Chevaliers bannerets" under Philip Augustus.

[6] The Chamberlain of France since 1205 had been Walter II of Villebéon, who died shortly after 1219 in the Holy Land. His son, Adam de Villebéon, became in his turn Chamberlain in 1223 and died in 1238.

[7] The brother of William of Belmont (or Beaumont), Bishop of Angers, was probably Richard, Viscount of Belmont and Lord of Sainte-Suzanne, who died in battle at Gaza in 1239.

[8] John of Arcis is referred to by Alberic des Trois Fontaines as Joannes de Arceis, and by the chronicle of Liége as de Archi. He had with him an illegitimate son, André of Espeissis. The father had been with King Philip at the battle of Bouvines. He fought so bravely at the tower that he was called *Berris*, probably a corruption of the Arabic *Bariz*, "a warrior more brave than others."

[9] Henry had already been on the crusades at the taking of Constantinople, and had taken home many stolen relics.

shal of the Hospital of Saint John,[10] and certain other brothers of the same House. Nor did the House of the Teutons escape without loss. The army of the Temple, which is usually first to assemble, was last to retreat. Therefore, when it arrived last at our ramparts, it stayed without, so that it might bring those who were before it back within the walls as soon as it was possible. Our persecutors finally returned to lead off the captives and to gather their spoils, presenting, as we afterwards learned from a Saracen, five hundred heads of Christians to the Sultan. Gloom took possession of our men, but not despair. For we know that this affliction was the punishment of sin, and that there was less in the punishment than our fault demanded, since He tempered the chastisement Who says to the soul of the sinner, "Thou hast prostituted thyself to many lovers; nevertheless return to me, and I will receive thee." [11] But it is clear to us that the unbelievers sustained grievous losses in their own picked army. That day "was the day of our tribulation, and of divine rebuke." [12] Truly the Lord is merciful Who "does not forget to show mercy, and in His anger will not shut up His mercies, Who in time of tribulation forgiveth sins; Who commanded light to shine out of darkness; Who turns our mourning into joy," [13] our sorrow into gladness. For the Sultan, sending one of our captives, began to negotiate with us concerning peace or a truce, during which negotiation we promptly repaired our ramparts and other fortifications.

CHAPTER 30

Meanwhile the sailors, who were betrayers of Christianity, and with them very many pilgrims whose love of themselves was greater than their compassion for their brethren, before the time of the

[10] The Marshal of the Hospital was Aymar de Layron, who had been lord of Caesarea, 1193–1213, by marriage with Julianne, Lady of Caesarea. He entered the Hospital, probably at the death of Julianne, and appears as Marshal thereof during the Fifth Crusade. Although Oliver's statement is ambiguous, we may assume that Aymar was killed at this time as he never appears thereafter.
[11] Jeremias 3:1.
[12] IV Kings 19:3.
[13] Psalms 76:9; Tobias 3:13; II Corinthians 4:6; Esther 13:17.

accustomed passage, left the soldiers of Christ in the greatest danger; hoisting their sails and leaving port, they afforded dejection to us and courage to the Babylonians.

Interrupting our arrangement of peace on the vigil of Saints Cosmas and Damian and on the following feast day [Sept. 26–28] and even on the next Saturday, with galleys and barbots on the river, and with mangonels,[1] shields, and tree-trunks for filling in the ditch on land, they attacked us with their usual barbaric ferocity and violence. But the Mighty Warrior, the "Triumpher in Israel," [2] using His customary kindness, defended His camp, sending Savary of Mauléon [3] over the sea with armed galleys and very many warriors in this crisis of distress; and we, crying out to heaven, did not hesitate to rush into battle, but manfully stood our ground, killing, and forcing the enemy, wounded and confused, to withdraw from his three-day attack by the power of Him Who saves those who trust in Him.

CHAPTER 31

Meanwhile the city, being grievously afflicted by the long siege, by sword, famine, and pestilence, even more than can be written, placed its hope solely in the peace which the Sultan had promised the citizens. For famine had grown so strong in it that desirable foods were lacking, although spoiled foods abounded. For the grain of Egypt is not lasting on account of the soft earth in which it grows, except in the higher lands around Babylon where it is skillfully preserved for years; and as we heard, one fig was sold there for eleven besants. Because of the distress of the famine, various kinds of diseases harassed them; among the other grievances which

[1] A military engine used formerly for throwing stones, javelins, etc.
[2] I Kings 15:29.
[3] Savary of Mauléon, in Poitou, son of Ralph de Mauléon, helped the Count of Toulouse in the quarrel between France and England. Later he served in the English army. In 1224 he helped defend La Rochelle against Louis VIII. Finally he made homage to the French king, and was made governor of the islands near La Rochelle. He resisted the regent during the minority of St. Louis and died in 1233. He was also a celebrated poet, but not of any great ability, according to the *Histoire Littéraire de la France*, XVIII (Paris, 1895), p. 671.

they suffered, they were said to see nothing at night, as if struck by blindness, though their eyes were open. The Sultan, dissuading them from surrender, deceived the wretched men from day to day by empty promises. Finally, however, they blockaded their gates from within so that no one, coming to us from their number, might tell us how the days of affliction beset them. But any who could escape through the postern gate or down the walls by ropes clearly proved the distress of their people by their swollen and famished condition. The supply of bread and fodder began to diminish even for those who were besieging us from without in the army of the Saracens. For the Nile, which usually overflows from after the feast of Saint John the Baptist [June 24] until the Exaltation of the Holy Cross [Sept. 14] and irrigates the plains of Egypt, did not rise this year according to its custom, to the mark which the Egyptians usually place, but, as we learned, left a great part of the land dry, which could not be ploughed or sown at the proper season. Therefore the Sultan, fearing dearth and famine, and also because of his desire to keep Damietta, offered the Christians a peace with Coradin his brother on these terms: that he would give back the Holy Cross [1] which had formerly been captured in the victory of Saladin, along with the Holy City and all the captives who could be found alive throughout the kingdom of Babylon and Damascus, and also funds to repair the walls of Jerusalem; in addition he would restore the kingdom of Jerusalem entirely, except Krak and Montréal,[2] for the possession of which he would offer tribute for as long as the truce would last.

Now these are two places located in Arabia, which have seven very strong fortresses through which merchants of the Saracens and of the pilgrims, going to Mecca or returning from it, usually

---

[1] The crusaders often carried a relic of the Cross into battle. Many complained that Baldwin II endangered its safety by dangerous expeditions. It was lost by the Christians in the crushing defeat at the Horns of Hattin, July 4, 1187, but another part remained in the hands of the Christians. (See p. 14.)

[2] The castles of Krak and Montréal were located in the desert east of the Dead Sea. They commanded the caravan route between Syria and the south and were a constant menace to the Moslems when held by Christians. It was from them that Renaud de Chatillon had waged his campaigns against Saladin in the 1170's and 1180's. These fortresses had been a thorn in the flesh of the Moslems since their construction under Baldwin I, and they had no intention of ever letting them fall into Christian hands again.

cross; and whoever holds them in his power can very seriously injure Jerusalem with her fields and vineyards when he wishes. The King and the French and the Count of Chester with the leaders of the Germans firmly believed that this arrangement was of advantage to Christianity, and ought to be accepted; and it was not to be marveled at, since they would have been satisfied with the much more insignificant peace which was formerly offered, had they not been opposed by wise counsel. But the Legate, with the Patriarch, the archbishops and bishops, the Templars and Hospitallers, and all the leaders of Italy [3] and many other prudent men, effectively resisted this arrangement, showing reasonably that Damietta ought to be taken before everything. Difference of opinion produced discord which was quickly settled because of the common need. Meanwhile the Sultan secretly sent a great multitude of foot soldiers through the marshy places to the city on the Sunday night after the feast of All Saints [Nov. 2–3]; two hundred and forty of them attacked the palisades while the Christians were sleeping; but the outcry of the sentries roused us, and about two hundred or more, according to our count, were killed or captured.

CHAPTER 32

On November fifth, in the reign of the Savior of the world, and with Pelagius, Bishop of Albano, skillfully and vigilantly executing the office of Legate of the Apostolic See, Damietta was captured without treachery, without resistance, without violent pillage and tumult, so that the victory may be ascribed to the Son of God alone, Who inspired His people to the entrance of Egypt and administered help there. And when the city was captured before the eyes of the King of Babylon, he did not dare, according to his usual custom, to attack through our rampart the soldiers of Christ who were prepared for the attack. At the same time also the river overflowed, filling our ditch with copious water. But the Sultan himself, in con-

[3] The Italians had their minds fixed upon the commercial advantages which would result to Pisa, Genoa, and Venice from possession of the delta by Europeans. Hence their opposition to the lifting of the siege of Damietta. Oliver's partisanship for Pelagius is evident in his treatment of this episode.

fusion, burned his own camp and fled. But God, Who on the third day gathered the waters under the firmament into one place, Who Himself brought His soldiers through the waters of the sea to the harbor of Damietta on the third day of the month of May, led them over the Nile to besiege the city on the third day of the month of February, and Himself captured Damietta located amidst the waters, on the third day of the month of November.

We can liken this city, which was overthrown by a third shaking of the earth, to a destroying bull; we call it "bull" because of its wantonness. For because of its fishes, birds, and pastures, grain, gardens, and orchards, it grew rich by trading and by practising piracy. It has overflowed with delights in its guilt, it has overflowed in hell. "But in one hour has thy judgment come." [1] We say "destroying" because its inhabitants perished in the third shaking of the earth, yet it remained unharmed itself. It was first besieged by the Greeks and Latins who finally went away from it; [2] next by the Latins under Amalric, King of Jerusalem, who were not successful; [3] but this third time, the "King of kings and Lord of lords" [4] delivered it to His servants; Jesus Christ, Who conquers and reigns and commands, "Who for the Egyptians has dried up everything sown by the water, and hath confounded them that wrought in flax and silk, combing and weaving fine cloth." [5] With this Leader, the soldiers of Christ, attacking Damietta, found its streets strewn with the bodies of the dead, wasting away from pestilence and famine; very much gold and silver, silk stuffs of the merchants in abundance, various household goods in superabundance. In addition to the natural location of the place, by which it is fortified, this city is surrounded by a triple wall, stoutly protected by many large brick towers; it is the key to all Egypt, and its protection is well located between Raamses and the field of Tanis in the land of

[1] Apocalypse 18:10.
[2] In the autumn of 1169 Constantinople supplied many ships for King Amalric I (1162–74) and his army. Shortage of food and bad weather helped to terminate the unsuccessful siege in December of the same year.
[3] Oliver is confused on these campaigns. The Greeks and Amalric were together in the siege of 1169 (see preceding note). Amalric's earlier campaigns took place in 1163 and 1167.
[4] Apocalypse 19:16.
[5] Isaias 19:7–9.

Gessen,[6] as we can surmise because there is the pasture land which the sons of Israel sought from Pharaoh at the time of famine.[7]

CHAPTER 33

Damietta! renowned among kingdoms, very famous in the pride of Babylon, ruler of the sea, plunderer of Christians, seized in the pride of your persecutors by means of a few small ladders, now you are "humbled under the mighty hand of God";[1] and casting out the adulterer whom you kept for a long time, you have returned to your former husband; and you who first brought forth bastards, now shall bear legitimate sons for the faith of the Son of God, being firmly held by the faithful of Christ. The Bishop of Acre[2] released from you the first fruits of souls for God by cleansing in the sacramental waters of baptism your little ones, who were found in you, alive by His power, even though they were near death. You have been subjected to manifold punishments because besides those who were taken alive in you, your dead of both sexes from the time of the siege round about you are computed at thirty thousand and more. The Lord struck them down without sword and fire, scorning henceforth to endure the uncleanness committed in you.

CHAPTER 34

Therefore let the universal Church rejoice by returning worthy acts of thanksgiving for such a triumph, and not only for Damietta, but for the destruction of the dangerous fortress of Mount Tabor and for our free approach into Jerusalem, that its walls may be rebuilt at the time foreseen by the Most High; besides, for the Castle of the Son of God, which the army of the Temple, at great expense, is making useful and impregnable, concerning which we have written more fully above. Rejoice, province of Cologne, exult and give praise, because in ships, instruments of war, warriors and

---

[6] This is inaccurate, for both Raamses and Tanis are south of Damietta.
[7] *See* Genesis 47.

---

[1] I Peter 5:6.
[2] Jacques de Vitry is portrayed as doing the same at Mount Tabor. (*See* p. 16.)

weapons, supplies and money, you have given more aid than the rest of the entire German kingdom! Our illustrious Emperor and King of Sicily is being eagerly awaited by the people of God for the happy consummation of the enterprise. Thou, O Cologne, city of saints, who dwellest in the gardens of the roses of martyrs, of the lilies of virgins, of the violets of confessors,[1] now rejoicing in a temporal peace through our venerable Archbishop, because of the devotion of thy daughters, bend the knees of thy heart before the Most High, Who has power of life and death. "Be not high minded, but in His sight fear, reprove your ways, lest the wrath of God which hath fallen upon thee"[2] be turned into hail, but . . . since peaceful times have long been granted, serve Him with a free mind, to Whom is honor and excellence, might and power.[3]

CHAPTER 35

Before the capture of Damietta there came to our attention a book written in Arabic, in which the author says that he was neither Jew nor Christian nor Saracen. But whoever he was, he predicted the evils which Saladin cruelly brought upon the Christian people in the destruction of Tiberias, and in the victory which he had over the Christians when he took captive the King of Jerusalem and its princes, occupied the Holy City, and destroyed Ascalon; it also predicted how he tried to seize Tyre but did not succeed, and many other things which the sins of that time deserved.[1] He also foretold the destruction of the gardens of the palm grove of the city of Damietta, which we saw had been accomplished when we examined this book through an interpreter. He also added that Damietta

[1] See Canticle of Canticles 6:1–2.
[2] Romans 11:20; Job 13:15; II Paralipomenon 34:21.
[3] Five manuscripts give this reading, instead of the words "Our illustrious Emperor," etc.: "But you, Cologne, city of saints, who dwell in gardens among the lilies of virgins, the roses of martyrs, the violets of confessors, bend the knees of your heart for the devotion of your daughters, and intone glorious acts of thanksgiving in lofty words."

[1] The prophecies themselves may be read in *Quinti Belli Sacri Scriptores Minores*, II, ed. Röhricht (Genevae, 1879), where they are given as *La Prophétie de Hannan* (pp. 206–13), and *Prophetia Filii Agap* (pp. 214–28).

would be captured by the Christians; he does not use the name of Saladin, but points him out by means of his black eyes and saffron banners. Besides, he predicted that a certain king [2] of the Christian Nubians was to destroy the city of Mecca and cast out the scattered bones of Mohammed, the false prophet, and certain other things which have not yet come to pass. If they are brought about, however, they will lead to the exaltation of Christianity and the suppression of the Agarenes.[3] We know that certain heathen gentiles had the Holy Spirit on their lips, but not in their heart, and prophesied plainly about Christ; therefore we are not surprised if purer water flows through stone channels.

Besides this, a report, spreading through the whole world, that Damietta had been captured by the Christians, caused a letter of the Georgians to be sent to the camp of the Catholics. It said that that nation, angered and roused by shame, decreed and swore, as the king convoked the leaders, that she would besiege some famous city of the Saracens, alleging that she would be ashamed because the Franks, coming from regions across the sea, and from the uttermost bounds of the earth, over a vast ocean full of dangers, had captured so well fortified a city by a long siege, unless they themselves, for whom it was easier to attack the enemy, should capture Damascus, or another specified place, by the strength of their arms. Now the Georgians are believers in Christ, and are neighbors to

[2] A legendary Eastern priest and king of the race of the Magi was Prester John, often referred to by late medieval historians. The first authentic mention of him is made in 1145 by Otto of Freising in his Chronicle. When Damietta was conquered in 1221, the victors spread a report that in the East, King David, either the son or the nephew of Prester John, had started with three strong armies against the Mohammedans. An Arabic prophecy foretold that Islam would be abolished when Easter fell on April 3. When this happened in 1222, many thought that King David (referred to here by Oliver) and his forces would join the expected army of Frederick II. Enthusiasm over this hope helped lead to the premature outbreak against Cairo and the defeat of the crusaders. The origin of the name David has not been satisfactorily explained, but the story has an historical kernel in that about this time Jenghiz Khan led three groups and destroyed the Mohammedan power in inner Asia.

[3] The Saracens were often referred to as Agarenes during the Middle Ages. Marbury B. Ogle, "Petrus Comestor, Methodius and the Saracens," *Speculum* XXI (1946), 318–24, points out that the tradition of ecclesiastical historians, influenced by St. Jerome's rendering of the Chronicle of Eusebius, very often referred to Saracens as Agarenes because of their reputed descent from Agar, the handmaid of Abraham.

the Persians, separated from the Land of Promise by a long stretch of country; their kingdom extends as far as the Caspian Mountains, in which ten tribes enclosed (there) await the time of anti-Christ, for then they will burst forth and will cause great destruction. The Georgians are warlike men, having the tonsure on their heads, round for the clergy, and square for the laity. Their women of the noble class are trained for battle. When those men are going to attack the enemy in orderly array, each one drinks a small gourd filled with pure wine, and at once they attack their adversaries courageously.

We do not doubt that it is to be counted among the favors of Christ our Protector, that He defended our leaders from the murderers of our persecutors in the siege of Damietta. For the Assassins [4] and their chief, the Old Man of the Mountains,[5] had the custom of casting knives against the Christians to cut off the lives of those who care for the business of Christianity. For at the time of the truce they wantonly killed the son of the Count of Tripoli,[6] a fine young man, who was prostrate before the altar in the church of the Blessed Virgin at Tortosa; wherefore the army of the Temple did not cease to pursue them for such a violation of religious liberty, until they were humiliated to the servitude of paying a tribute of three thousand besants annually to the Templars.

[4] The secret order of Assassins had been founded by a Persian named Hassan late in the 11th century. Though they originally killed the enemies of their brand of Islam, they later killed for political reasons and made themselves feared throughout the East. Their first location was Alamut, near the Caspian Sea, but they later gained a series of fortresses in Lebanon.

[5] The leader of the Assassins was known to the Christians as the Old Man of the Mountains. His power was very extensive, for he had at his disposal a fanatical band of experts in murder. Even Saladin felt compelled to treat with him. As the Old Man was supposed to live forever and the elections to the office were held in the greatest secrecy, the names of but few of these rulers are known.

[6] Bohemond IV, the One-Eyed, was first Regent, then (from 1199) Count of Tripoli. By his first wife, Plaisance of Gibelet, he had a son Raymond who is here referred to.

CHAPTER 36

At the time of the siege, Leo, King of Armenia, died at a good old age.[1] Likewise the Sultan of Iconium [2] died. He is believed to have been baptized, and was so kindly disposed toward the Christians that when making war on the side of the Saracens he ordered the followers of Christ to be released whom he found in chains in the fortification which he attacked. He gave them their choice of returning into their own country, if they wished, or of receiving money from him and waging war under him if they preferred. So familiar was he with Christians, that he made them guardians of his own person, although his father had been killed by Lascaris the Greek.[3] He also supported Miralis,[4] the disinherited son of Saladin, against the sons of Saphadin, as far as the Caliph of Baghdad, pope of his own race, permitted.

Melchiseraph,[5] son of Saphadin, inflicted many losses on the Templars when they were in the siege of Damietta; for he burned

[1] Leo II, the Great, 1187 (crowned 1189)–1219. With the help of the Hospitallers he had dispossessed 'Izz-al-Dîn I of Iconium of the cities of Heraclea and Laranda in southeast Cappadocia in 1211. When John of Brienne in 1212 lost his first wife, Marie de Montferrat, Leo's daughter Stephanie was given to him in marriage.

[2] 'Izz-al-Dîn Kaikâwus I, a Seljuk, Sultan of Iconium, 1210–19. In 1216 he took full revenge on Leo for the loss of Laranda by crushing the Armenian army under the Constable Constantine and capturing the leader along with many Armenian nobles. To ransom these captives, Leo had not only to restore Laranda, but also to cede the region of Bozanti and Ermaneksu in Isauria. Sultan 'Ala-al-Dîn Kaîqubâd I (1219–37), his successor, took from the Armenians all the rest of Isauria except Selefke. The mistaken belief that some Mohammedan leaders were ready for conversion made Oliver write in 1221 a letter to the "King of Babylon" urging him to become a Christian and another to the "Doctors of Egypt" at the same time.

[3] In the spring of 1211 Theodore Lascaris killed Sultan Kaîkhosru of Iconium in battle.

[4] When Saladin died in 1186, his oldest son, Malik-al-Afdal (known to the Latins as Miralis), succeeded him at Damascus, in southern Syria, and in Palestine. In 1196 he was overthrown by his uncle, Saphadin, who also seized the throne of Egypt in 1200 from another nephew, Malik-al-'Aziz.

[5] Malik-al-Aschraf, son of Saphadin, helped overthrow his nephew Al-Malik en-Nasser Salah-ed-Dîn Dawoud in 1228, and succeeded him at Damascus. He died August 27, 1237.

the town of Safita,⁶ and destroyed its fortified towers. But when he returned to his own land, he was conquered by the Saracens. At the same time Bohemond, Count of Tripoli, attacking Antioch, forcibly ejected Rupen, a certain kinsman of his, from the rule of that city,⁷ choosing rather to have the pleasure of a temporal sin than to be afflicted along with the Christian people. Therefore the Legate of the Apostolic See officially proclaimed the sentence of excommunication and interdict against him and Tripoli and the lands in which he committed the crime.

CHAPTER 37

"The Lord hath broken the staff of the wicked. He hath broken the horn of the proud; He Who above the sons of men is terrible," ¹ has powerfully opened the gates of Damietta. As we were entering it, there met us an intolerable odor, a wretched sight. The dead killed the living. Man and wife, father and son, master and slave, killed each other by their odor. Not only were the streets full of the dead, but in the houses, in the bedrooms, and on the beds lay the corpses. When a husband had perished, a woman, powerless to rise and lacking the help of one to support her, died, not being able to bear the odor; a son near his father or vice versa, a handmaid beside her mistress or vice versa, wasted away with illness and lay dead. "Little ones asked for bread and there was none to break it for them," ² infants hanging at the breasts of their mothers opened

---

⁶ Safita, or Chastel-Blanc, is southeast of Tortosa. In Chapter 42 of Oliver, Coradin (Al-Malik al-Moadden), son of Saphadin, is rightly mentioned as its destroyer. The place was known to Greek writers as Argyrokastron, and belonged to the Templars. Saladin gained possession of it before he died, and Coradin demolished it, as mentioned here, in 1219 or 1220. It was again fortified by the Templars in 1246 or 1247, and was finally conquered by Baibars in 1271.

⁷ Bohemond IV, the One-Eyed (*see* p. 51, n. 6), with the aid of Templars, seized the rule of Antioch from his nephew Rupen-Raymond, the son of his older brother and the daughter of Leo of Armenia. Leo championed his grandson. Twice Rupen was installed in Antioch by Armenian arms, but he was finally driven out, and died trying to assert his claims to the throne of Armenia.

---

¹ Isaias 14:5; Psalms 74:11; 65:5.
² Lamentations 4:4.

their mouths in the embrace of one dead. Fastidious rich men died of hunger amid piles of wheat, those foods being lacking by which they had been raised; in vain did they desire melons and garlic, onions, fish and fowl, fruits of the tree and herbs. In them was fulfilled the prophecy of the prophet: "Instead of a sweet smell there shall be stench, as rotten carcass shall not have company in burial."[3] Almost eighty thousand, as we learned from the report of captives, perished in the city from the beginning of the siege to its end: all except those whom we found, healthy or ill, about three thousand in number. Three hundred of these, the more notable ones of both sexes, were kept for the ransom of our captives; some died after the victory, others were sold for a great price, and others were baptized and given to Christ.

CHAPTER 38

This city fortified in degrees had its first wall low for the protection of the ditch, the second one higher, the third loftier than the second. The middle wall has twenty-eight main towers containing two or three tortoises [1] each, which all remained unharmed along with the walls, except one which was considerably shattered by the frequent blows of the trebuchet of the Duke of Austria. For our army was so given over to dissipation that the knights devoted themselves to leisure, neglecting the work of God, while the common people turned to the taverns and to fraudulent dealings. Two cats [2] had been made at great expense to fill the ditch. One of them in the custody of the King, the other in the custody of the Romans, were burned when the guardians of the city were still powerful in arms. Two subterranean ditches were made to undermine the foundations of the fortifications; but that labor was frustrated after very much expense. The Lord wished to give the city unharmed, without loss of those capturing it, and that by reason of His power. We all swore in common that the spoils carried off from the city

[3] Isaias 3:24; 14:19–20.

[1] A sort of penthouse under which fighters were protected, as a tortoise by its shell.
[2] A kind of low movable defensive structure used in medieval warfare in approaching fortifications. Called also cat house, cat castle, and rat.

should be given up to be divided among the victors; this also was enjoined under terrible anathema by the Legate of the Apostolic See. Transgressors will remain to be reckoned in disgrace forever with Achan,[3] who at Jericho took something of what had been anathematized. Truly the concupiscence of the eyes made many men thieves. Nevertheless we received for the benefit of the state a great part of the luxuries of Egypt, in gold and silver, pearls and apples of amber, golden threads and various fringes, precious silken stuffs, as Isaias enumerates: "In that day he will take away the ornaments of shoes, and little moons, and chains and necklaces, and bracelets and bonnets, and bodkins and ornaments of the legs, and tablets and sweet balls and earrings, and rings and jewels hanging on the forehead, and changes of apparel, and short cloaks and fine linen and crisping pins, and looking-glasses, and lawns and headbands, and fine veils," [4] which no one could list in full. But we are spending much time in considering them. These things were distributed through the army of the Lord with grain which was found in the city.

CHAPTER 39

The Legate of the Apostolic See joined Damietta, with all her dependents and belongings, to the Kingdom of Jerusalem forever. The mosque of Damietta, through the invocation of the holy and undivided Trinity, was converted into a church of the blessed and glorious Virgin Mary. Being built in square form, we can see almost as much of its width as we can of its length. It is supported by one hundred and forty-one marble columns, having seven porticoes, and in the middle a long wide-open space in which a pyramid ascends on high in the manner of a ciborium; beyond the west side a tower rises after the manner of a campanile. Four main altars are built in it: the first under the title of Blessed Mary; the second of Peter, the Prince of the Apostles; the third of the Holy Cross; the fourth of blessed Bartholomew, on whose feast the tower in the river was captured.

[3] *See* Josue 7.
[4] Isaias 3:18–23.

In Damietta were found four trebuchets with petraries and many mangonels; very strong ballistae with a lathe; on account of the multitude we do not know the number of hand ballistae and bows. Every kind of equipment for brave men that was found was kept for Christianity. Gold and silver, with pearls and other things easy to move, were divided proportionally not only among clerics and knights, but also among attendants, women, and children. The towers of the city with its homes were distributed among the kingdoms whose warriors had assembled for its capture; one tower was in the first place reserved, as was right and fitting, and was assigned to the Roman Church, with its gate, which formerly was called the Babylonian but now is called the Roman. Another tower also was reserved for the Archbishop of Damietta; and as formerly Jerusalem, the Holy City of the living God, was captured by the enemy at night, so the Christians obtained Damietta before dawn. The machine by which the tower of the river had been captured, the Germans and Frisians donated in common, and out of it was made a new bridge between the city and the fort which is constructed as a defense of the bank opposite the city. Two small fortresses were placed together for the protection of the bridge, by the same machine. Besides, from other trees on which the ladders hung, a watch place was set up on the summit of the new fort to point out the harbor to those sailing at a distance. An old bridge, which with an island in the middle touched both banks, had been attacked many times by the Saracens at the time of siege, and had been manfully defended by the Christians. Having done its work, it is kept for other uses.

CHAPTER 40

By no less a miracle, but rather by a greater one did the Lord give to the Christians the fort of Tanis,[1] in the month of November, on the feast of blessed Clement [Nov. 23] who has his dwelling on the sea. For scouts were sent, about a thousand in number, in small ships through the little river which is called the Tanis, so that they might take food supplies for themselves from the casalia and care-

---

[1] The biblical Taphnis, near Pelusium at the eastern border of Lower Egypt.

fully explore the location of the aforesaid place. The Saracens, who were in the garrison of the fort, seeing the Christians and thinking that the whole army was arriving, fled after locking the doors. But our men, having Christ alone as their leader there, breaking through the barriers, entered the fort. Returning they declared to us that never had they seen a stronger fort on a plain; it had seven very strong towers, fortified by tortoises, and a breastwork; and besides it was surrounded by a twofold ditch, each part of which is protected by a wall. A lake stretches out in breadth round about to such an extent that approach is impossible to our horsemen in winter, and so difficult in summer that it would never be taken by our army in siege. The lake abounds in fish, and from its fisheries four thousand silver marks were paid annually to the Sultan of Babylon, as was told to us by elders; besides, it abounds in birds and salt works; many casalia round about were subject to it. The city beyond the fort, greater than Damietta, once famous but now in ruins, bears witness to the size of its buildings. This is Tanis, whose field the prophet mentions: "Wonderful things did he do in the sight of their fathers," [2] and Isaias: "Many princes of Tanis, the wise counselors of Pharaoh, have given foolish counsel." [3] This is Tanis, in which Jeremias is said to have been stoned. For when Jerusalem had been destroyed by the Babylonians,[4] and Godolias had been killed by Ishmael,[5] the rest of the people against the counsel of Jeremias set out into Egypt, taking with them Jeremias, who remained with them in Tanis, "and the word of the Lord was made known to Jeremias in Tanis: 'Take great stones and hide them in the vault that is under the brick wall at the gate of Pharaoh's house,' " [6] etc. Afterwards Jeremias said to them: "Thus sayeth the Lord: I have sworn by My great Name . . . that all the men of Juda that are in the land of Egypt shall perish by sword and by famine until they be wholly consumed." [7] And the people rose against Jeremias, and they stoned him with the stones which had been hidden under the brick wall. But the Egyptians honored the

[2] Psalms 77:12.
[3] Isaias 19:11.
[4] *See* Jeremias 52.
[5] Jeremias 41.
[6] Jeremias 43:8–9.
[7] Jeremias 44:26–27.

prophet, burying him next to the tomb of their kings, being mindful of the benefits which he had shown to Egypt. For by his words he had driven away the beasts of the waters, which the Greeks call crocodiles. Now Alexander the Macedonian, coming to the tomb of the prophet and being acquainted with the mystery of the place, transferred him to Alexandria and buried him gloriously.[8] But we found and killed crocodiles at Damietta. Now this beast is cruel, devouring men and animals, and it cares for its eggs simply by watching them with its eyes open. Its young, being hatched, flee the parent as an enemy; for in an instant it gulps down and devours whomever it can snatch.

Tanis is separated from Damietta by a journey of one day over the sea in the direction of the Land of Promise, so that it is easy to place a garrison there or to send food from Acre or from Damietta, across the sea or over land or by river. It caused many losses to the Christians in the siege of Damietta, when ships approaching us or going away from us were carried there by the force of the winds. For before Tanis, the coast, which is curved and without harbors, makes a wide, full bay; and ships drifting into it cannot withdraw without a wind that is highly favorable to them.

CHAPTER 41

Coradin, having returned from Egypt into Palestine, besieged the castle of Caesarea, which was in the custody of the King, and in a short time he captured and destroyed it while its defenders acted negligently; nevertheless they almost all escaped because they had a free entrance and exit over the sea. Next he proceeded to the Castle of the Son of God with all his army, and regarding it from every direction, he shrewdly realized that it could not be seized; besides he found the Templars prepared for every danger; for they had reinforced the camp with provisions and with all the equipment of brave men. At the same time the Templars manfully drove back the bandits of the Saracens from Acre by killing some and

---

[8] There is no mention of this in Curtius Rufus. Nothing certain is known about the last days of Jeremias. A Christian tradition states that he was stoned at Taphnis. It seems to begin with Tertullian.

capturing others. But Coradin demanded help from the Saracens, so that coming from the east they might besiege Acre, a thing which he could not accomplish because of the constant discord of the princes of the land themselves, which was highly favorable to the Christians, and which the Caliph, their pope, labored to quiet.

CHAPTER 42

In the year of the Incarnate Word 1220, Coradin, Prince of Damascus, destroyed Safita.[1] Now this was the strongest fort of the Templars, which Saladin, the scourge of the Christians, reduced by a long siege to such a point that the defenders, wasting away with hunger, and having obtained the permission of the Master of the army of the Temple, surrendered it to the tyrant. What voice, what tongue can repeat for us the benefits of our Savior, multiplied without us? They are benefits of Him Whom an inherent goodness and natural clemency, and also the continued supplication of the church, have induced to look with a kindly eye upon the camp of the faithful because of the sweetness of their devotion! A plea softens Him, a tear forces Him, and how can the hand of a writer or the tongue of a speaker be sufficient for Him for Whose praise a conscience remaining quiet in the heart is not sufficient? However, it is pleasing to heap up and admire the marvels wrought in a short space of time which descended from the Father of Lights. The sons of Israel were at hand, going about with the ark of the Lord, sounding their sackbuts and shouting, on the seventh day, when the walls of Jericho fell, so that the people of the Lord might have free entrance.[2] But we slept before Damietta, cowardly and sluggish, benumbed and given ever to idleness; none the less, the walls of Jerusalem fell, and those of Mount Tabor, Safita, and the other fortifications opposing in a hostile way; besides, the Most High, against the will of certain false Christians, gave us Damietta. To this, from the treasure of His generosity He added the impregnable fort of Tanis with its supply of provisions in a hostile land—He

---

[1] Here Oliver corrects his error of Chapter 36.
[2] Josue 6:11–20.

Who rained manna from heaven upon His believers in the desert. It is therefore clear to all, through the evidence of miracle, that this holy pilgrimage is pleasing and acceptable to God. May they blush and be confounded who received the rewards of the Supreme King from His Church, and, fighting indifferently or retreating before time, corrupted His pilgrimage; they will give an account to the Judge Who cannot be either corrupted or deceived. Let the sluggish be aroused, who have not yet carried out their vow. For "it is ruin to a man to devour holy ones, and after vows, to retract." [3] What excuse will they offer on the day of tribulation and distress, who took away the labors of others,[4] killing souls to which preachers of the truth have given life; who had regard for their own avarice and took the sign of the Cross from the shoulders of the wretched, whom they made transgressors of their vow? Let them also return to wisdom whom guilt accuses and conscience convicts of this, that by alleging false reasons of poverty and debility, they have cheated the religion of those who have been examined, because only the judgment of God is according to truth. But the defrauders of the alms which were collected for the aid of the Holy Land, because they have concealed their fault by lying to the Holy Ghost, shall perish and have their lot with Ananias and Saphira;[5] and with Judas, the most wicked thief and betrayer of his Lord, they shall be punished in hell because, though betrayers of Christianity, they kept for themselves the wages of fighting men, and gave their souls for transitory things. Cupidity has caused their theft and they are unmindful of Jerusalem our mother, who, lying prostrate on the ground, desires to be lifted up from her Babylonian captivity by those who are returning. Be consoled, "city of God, because nations from afar shall come to thee, and bearing gifts, shall adore the Lord in thee; they shall be cursed who despised thee, and they shall be condemned that have blasphemed thee. The blessed that built thee up shall rejoice. But thou shalt rejoice in thy children, and blessed are all they that love thee and that rejoice in thy peace."[6]

---

[3] Proverbs 20:25.
[4] *See* Ezechiel 23:29.
[5] Acts 5:9.
[6] Tobias 13:10–18.

CHAPTER 43

It happened when the year was changing, when kings usually set out to war, that John, King of Jerusalem, left the camp of the faithful.[1] He feigned many reasons for excusing himself and promised a speedy return, but forgetful of the past, he turned to the future. When the Lord opened His hand and filled the port of Damietta with abundance of grain, wine, and oil, and when a numerous band of pilgrims and horses had been added so that there might be no grounds of excuse for setting out upon an affair so happily begun, there arrived in the sixth passage the archbishops of Milan,[2] and Crete, the bishops of Faenza,[3] and Reggio,[4] and messengers of Frederick the King, bearing letters with golden seals and announcing his arrival. There was present the Bishop of Brescia[5] and a copious army of Italy. But the Legate considered that by a great privilege of grace and by divine bounty everything had been sufficiently attended to that the process of negotiation required; and he was struck with sorrow because time was passing away uselessly, and such a great opportunity was lost. Therefore, assembling the leaders, he, first of all, and after him the Archbishop of Milan, and other bishops likewise, strove to urge an advance against the Sultan who had pitched his camp on the Nile one day's journey from Damietta. But the knights, after holding a deliberation, spoke against this exhortation, pretending this reason above all—that the King of Jerusalem was away by voluntary choice, and no other prince was present whom the people of different nations were willing to obey to lead out the people of God—and thus they agreed upon inactivity, from which evils were multiplied in the camp.

[1] Probably at Easter, March 29. John had become constantly more irritated at the attitude of Pelagius. He used the affairs of Armenia as a pretext; he had married Stephanie, daughter of Leo II who died in 1219. John wished to claim the throne for himself in the name of his wife. Oliver explains John's Armenian aspirations in Chapter 45.
[2] Henry Septala, Archbishop of Milan, 1213–30.
[3] The Bishop of Crete is unknown. The Bishop of Faenza was Roland, 1210–21.
[4] Bishop Lando, 1216–34.
[5] Albert Rezzato, 1213–28.

CHAPTER 44

In the month of July came Count Matthew of Apulia [1] with eight galleys, two of which were corsairs that he had captured as they were threatening the Christians on the sea journey.

CHAPTER 45

Let the temerity of human presumption blush, which trusts erroneously in its own strength or in the strength of others, and clearly is very often confounded. This appeared in the case of the aforesaid Count. A previous report announced his arrival by frequent rumors, and, as if the negotiation would proceed only through him, its progress was hindered by delaying circumstances. But the memory of such great hope perished with a crash. It was not due to the Count that the hope was not carried through to its desired consequence, because, as the Legate witnessed, his will was prompt and the equipment which he had brought and which he afterwards added appeared magnificent to all and in complete accord with military knowledge. Besides he made a sojourn in the army that was useful and suitable to the position of a soldier of Christ. But after he arrived at Damietta, the Legate took counsel with any nation that was then in the camp who seemed to have the greatest zeal, and with Count Matthew himself, to whom an advance against the King of Babylon seemed advantageous. Next he called the princes and leaders of the multitude, and in a public address roused to labor a people who were sluggish and given over to idleness.

But the leaders, especially the Franks, spoke against this honorable exhortation, effectively inducing the Earl of Arundel,[1] a leader

---

[1] Matteo Gentile, referred to in a diploma of 1229 as *Matthaeus Gentilis comes Alesinae* (present day Lesina) *et civitatis capitaneus et magister justitiarius Apuliae et Terrae Laboris*. He had been placed in charge of Apulia by Emperor Frederick, at whose orders he came on the crusade.

---

[1] William, Earl of Arundel and Sussex. He was active in all the contests between John Lackland and the French king. He died in Italy in 1220 or 1221 after his return from the crusade.

among the English, and the more noble among the Germans, to hinder the proposal of the Legate. Among other trifling reasons, the absence of King John was frequently alleged, who had acted contrary to the agreement which he had made at Acre when the pilgrims were about to sail into Egypt, that he would not desert them while he was alive and free. Contrary to his solemn agreement he returned to Acre; and not attending to the business of Christianity, he prepared himself and made a journey to Armenia.[2] For having as his wife the daughter of Leo, the deceased King of Armenia, he aimed at the dominion of that region, as it is said; but being frustrated in his hope, he was not received by the barons of Armenia. At almost the same time the Queen died, along with the King's little son. Rupen, Prince of Antioch, also sought this kingdom; a Catholicos,[3] primate of the aforesaid nation, powerfully besieged him in the city of Tarsus; he was taken and imprisoned, and died there. Now the Catholicos favored the younger daughter of King Leo,[4] to whom her father before his death made the princes of his kingdom swear fealty; he died a short time afterwards.

CHAPTER 46

The Legate, after frequent public and private admonitions, grieved that so numerous an army was stationary, and not progressing, and would be going back in the next passage; finally by his example of action, he began to urge others to join the retinue, causing his tents to be pitched in a flat place. However, the opposition of the leaders prevailed to such a degree that even some Gallic and Ger-

[2] See p. 61, n. 1.

[3] Catholicos is the title given to the heads of the Armenian, Georgian, and Nestorian churches. At first it designated a dignitary superior to a metropolitan, but inferior to a patriarch. Now the term means the same as patriarch usually, but present-day Armenians have three catholicoi and two patriarchs. The primacy of honor is given to the Catholicos of Etshmiadzin. The Catholicos at the time of Leo's death was John Medzabaro.

[4] Zabel was daughter of Leo II by his second wife, Sybille, daughter of Aymeri de Lusignan, king of Cyprus. She married Philip, son of Bohemond IV of Antioch and of Plaisance of Gibelet. Philip was put to death in prison by order of the Grand-Baron Constantine whose son Hayton then married Zabel (1224–25). Hayton exercised little power until the death of his father. He abdicated in 1270, and entered a monastery where he took the name of Macarius (see Chapter 87).

man mercenaries, who had accepted his money, hindered his plan of advancing. Certain of them were excommunicated, and others who were to be excommunicated afterwards were disturbed, and were compelled to return the pay that they accepted according to proportion of time. The Italian soldiers by vain hope cheated the religious zeal of the Legate, promising assistance for the advance, "but the sons of Ephraim, bending and shooting the bow, have turned back in the day of battle." [1] For while they were clearly regarding the persistence of the Legate and the boldness of the march against the Sultan, they agreed with the dissenters mentioned above, and opposed the advance, although the Christians did not lack an abundance of soldiers or attendants. Galleys were in abundance, barbots were prepared, a numerous multitude of archers was present, there was a plentiful supply of provisions, there was a suitable place between the river on the right and the lake on the left, as if the Lord were saying to us: "What is there I ought to do more to my vineyard and I have not done it? Was it that I looked that it should bring forth grapes and it hath brought forth wild grapes?" [2] For besides the other things which were provided by the Lord for the setting out of the expedition, as we learned from our scouts, the King of Babylon then had little aid, and a great multitude of Bedouins had joined us and would have given their wives and children as hostages if they had known that the Christians had undertaken the attempt manfully, as we learned through their letters and messengers. And this seemed probable because they are subject under tribute to the Sultan; indeed they formerly ruled in the land of Egypt until they were powerfully oppressed by Saladin and were scattered through the wilderness of the desert.

CHAPTER 47

The Legate after much weariness, because he had an unwilling retinue and especially because the river overflowed at that time,

[1] Psalms 77:9.
[2] Isaias 5:4.

withdrew to the previous camp, strongly urging the authors of the delay, in a public sermon, that the work of God, being happily begun, should not be ended and that they should judge themselves, lest they be grievously condemned by the Judge of secret things.

CHAPTER 48

No one can describe the corruption of our army after Damietta was given us by God, and the fortress of Tanis was added. Lazy and effeminate, the people were contaminated with chamberings and drunkenness, fornications and adulteries, thefts and wicked gains. Afterwards,[1] certain of our men set out for a day's march into hostile territory, bringing back captives, oxen, and horses. Then the Templars, with their own special following, advanced in a swift march to a town on the seacoast, which is called Broil,[2] and brought back many spoils—about one hundred camels, the same number of captives, horses, mules, oxen, and asses and goats, clothing and much household furniture, returning unharmed after two days. However, on account of a lack of water, many horses and mules died on the way, although the men themselves returned safe. The Teutonic House, with many others, met them for joy, but when they delayed behind the Templars (it is not fully known for what reason), the swift horsemen of the Turks made an attack on them at the sea. Terrified men from other nations fled from them, but the English, the Flemish, the Teutons, and Robert of Belmont[3] sustained the attack as they came upon them. The Preceptor and the Marshal of the same House, with many other brothers and about twenty secular knights, were captured. Many horses of those who fled to defend themselves were killed because our men went out, not for battle, but to meet the Templars, and therefore were without crossbowmen and archers.

[1] In July 1220. This was, for the time, the only advance that Pelagius could urge upon the army. Outside of this pillaging expedition, the army remained inactive for the rest of 1220 and until June 1221.
[2] Broil lies to the west of Damietta and is today called Burlus.
[3] Apparently from a different Belmont (de Bello Monte) from that used in the name of Viscount Richard (de Pulchro Monte) mentioned on p. 42 (n.7).

CHAPTER 49

In the month of August there reached Damietta fourteen galleys equipped and sent at the same time by the Doge of Venice,[1] which brought some help to the Christians. At the same time the King of Babylon armed thirty-three galleys which caused us inestimable loss. For they captured the merchant ships, along with the men themselves, which were bringing supplies to Damietta; they even took the pilgrims captive, plundering and burning the ships. Besides, they attacked a large ship which was bringing Count Henry of Schwerin,[2] and other Teutonic nobles who were coming to us. They, however, defended themselves manfully; and having killed and wounded many pirates they fortunately escaped, although they lost one vessel from the Teutonic House, with barley which Greek fire destroyed.

CHAPTER 50

Here we are forced to insert the account of an unfortunate mishap. Count Diether of Katzenellenbogen [1] left us before the time of the passage with a great multitude of pilgrims, although he was strongly urged and admonished by the Lord Legate not to board that ship if he wished to set out for Thessalonica, but to go in a smaller vessel with a few men without diminishing the army. But he, with the master of the ship and many pilgrims, stubbornly took up the journey, and therefore, the Legate of the Apostolic See excommunicated that accursed ship and all who were sailing on it. Falling among pirates near Cyprus, it was burned. However, the shipwrecked Count escaped, swimming away with a few men.

---

[1] Pietro Ziani, Doge of Venice, 1205–29.

[2] Henry I, the Lion, Duke of Saxony and Count of Schwerin, 1160–1227, known for his connection with the seizure of King Waldemar of Denmark in 1223. He was on the crusade from 1220, and had returned home by March 1222.

---

[1] Diether II, Count of Katzenellenbogen, 1219–44, son of Diether I, 1214–19. He returned home in 1222.

CHAPTER 51

The galleys of the Venetians and others being requested to hurry, set out rather belatedly from the port of Damietta, going to Rosetta and Alexandria after we had suffered losses at the hands of the Saracens in the manner mentioned above.

CHAPTER 52

Coradin, knowing our inactivity, gathered an army from Syria, and more completely destroyed Jerusalem, the city of the living God, though it had been destroyed before. He scattered the cisterns that had previously been filled, had the city's marble columns carried off to Damascus, and advancing through the mountains and fields of Palestine he laid waste its fruit-bearing trees and vines. The Templars, knowing that he wished to besiege the Castle of the Son of God, began to destroy the deserted tower of Destroit in the upper section. But he, coming upon them later, razed it to the ground, cutting down the fruitful garden placed before it; he finally besieged the fort with a multitude of Turks, extending the line of their tents from the river to the salt works. Now he derived this audacity from the fact that he knew that around the beginning of October the seventh passage had been so small; for we believe that not one hundred soldiers came to our aid then with military weapons and horses. But a great multitude of the people of Acre came to Damietta, being driven from their lands by the pronouncement of the church. From that number those were allowed to return whose poverty could be known to us; others returned without permission to the increase of their destruction; and still others returned to their own lands after extorting permission through fraud. But a few, who had a more rational attitude, remained with us in exile.

CHAPTER 53

Coradin, having established the siege, and fearing an attack from the camp, ordered a rampart to be made between the fort and his tents. He set up one trebuchet, three petraries, and four mangonels, and harassed the fortification night and day by blows of the machines. However, he could not move one stone from its place in the new towers and the middle wall. But the trebuchet of the camp, with a petrary and a mangonel placed next to it, battered and broke the trebuchet and the petrary of the enemy. In the residence of the Templars, moreover, four thousand warriors were fed daily, except those who at their own expense had come from Acre to defend us or to sell provisions. But the Legate in haste requested the Queen of Cyprus [1] and the Christians, and the barons of Syria, through messengers and letters, to aid the fortress of Christianity. The Master of the Temple,[2] with a tested army of Templars, was permitted by the Legate, because of such a great need, to return to the Castle, and prepared to fight with Coradin. The men of Cyprus brought a great supply of soldiers and funds. Bohemond,[3] likewise, and the Lord of Beirut,[4] Guy of Gibelet,[5] with other pullani,[6] quickly prepared themselves to help. Learning this through scouts and betrayers of the Christians, Coradin was struck with fear and basely withdrew from the siege, suffering great losses at the hands of those holding the Castle, both in men and in horses. Like a proud and arrogant man, he had threatened that he would take the Castle by a long siege; but divine power forced him to retreat after he burned his own camp around the beginning of November.

[1] Alice, widow of Hugh of Lusignan (see p. 12, n. 5). She was the daughter of Henry II, Count of Champagne, and Isabelle of Jerusalem.

[2] Peter de Montagu, brother of Eustorgius of Nicosia and Guérin, Master of the Hospital, succeeded William of Chartres as Master of the Temple at the death of William in 1219. He held office until 1229.

[3] Bohemond IV. (See p. 51, n. 6.)

[4] John d'Ibelin, lord of Beirut, 1177–1236, was the most influential baron in Jerusalem. He had been Regent of the kingdom, 1205–10, for his niece Marie (see J. L. LaMonte in *Byzantion* XII [1937], 417–48).

[5] Guy of Gibelet (between Tyre and Beirut) was the son of Hugh II, Lord of Gibelet, and Etienette, daughter of Henry of Milly, brother of Philip, Lord of Naplouse. Guy's sister (by the same union) was Plaisance, wife of Bohemond IV, Prince of Antioch. Guy succeeded his father as Lord of Gibelet when he was still a minor. He married Alice, former wife of Bohemond. He survived the disaster of the crusade, and helped Frederick against the Ibelins in 1228 (see Chapter 87).

[6] A name given the Syrian-born Franks. The term is sometimes used to refer to children of mixed Frankish-native alliances, but is more generally used, as here, to mean Franks native to Syria.

THE CAPTURE OF DAMIETTA

Now many of the defenders of the Castle were wounded and a few died. May the Most High protect this home, built to the honor of the Son of God, hateful to the Saracens, but lovely to the Christians, the breastwork of the city of Acre, as it were. May the custody of angels be upon its walls "even to the consummation of the world." [7] Truly, "we have faith in the Lord Jesus," [8] since He Who began to destroy the enemies of the Cross is steadfast in His grace, and will accomplish it at the time of His own good pleasure. For already we perceived a certain proof of divine vengeance; for in the siege of the Castle, as we learned from our scouts, and clearly saw, since corpses were strewn through the fields, three emirs were killed there, and two hundred Mamelukes [9] most skilled in arms; but there was no count of their archers, and of those who were dragging them along in their machines, and who were destroyed by our crossbowmen, three hundred in number. In one day also were killed one hundred and twenty horses of great value, among which was one, bought for fourteen thousand drachmas, which Seraphus,[10] Sultan of Aleppo, sent to a certain emir for a gift; besides, the Saracens also sustained many losses of other horses and camels. [11]

CHAPTER 54

In the month of November, Lord Frederick, son of the Emperor Henry,[1] was crowned Emperor in Rome under Pope Honorius, in the great harmony of state and priesthood, and in the peace of the

---

[7] Matthew 28:20.
[8] *See* Ephesians 3:11–12.
[9] Mamelukes were Turkish slaves purchased for service in the Army. The Egyptian dynasties that followed the Ayyubites are often called Mameluke dynasties, because the sultans were taken from the enfranchised slaves who made up the court and supplied officers to the Army.
[10] Al-Malik al-Aschraf, son of Al-Adil, called Seraphus by European writers. He received from his father Edessa and Ayyubide Greater Armenia. In 1220 he became protector of the kingdom of Aleppo for Al-Aziz, whom he protected against the Seljuks of Anatolia.
[11] *See* Appendix A, pp. 96–7.

[1] Frederick II of Hohenstaufen, son of Henry VI and Constance of Sicily. He had been crowned King of Sicily and of Germany previously; this was his coronation as Emperor in Rome.

Romans. Being signed with the Cross, he made ready to go to the assistance of the Holy Land, sending ahead the Duke of Bavaria,[2] who came to Damietta in the year 1221 in the eighth passage with the bishop of Passau,[3] the Marquis of Baden,[4] Count Guy of Brienne,[5] and other nobles in the month of May. The emperor committed his post to this leader until he should cross the sea in person. Then the Legate of the Apostolic See, considering the fitness of the time, and the cost of idleness, began to treat with the Duke again about the business of war, for the forwarding of which he had remained in Egypt. Besides, the aforesaid Duke urged that the multitude of the faithful should attack the camp of the Sultan, before the river should take up its usual increase. Therefore by the common plan of the barons, knights, and the common people we began to arrange tents up the river beyond the camp in the month of June on the feast of the apostles Peter and Paul [June 29]. It was known by the statement of the Bishop-elect of Beauvais and of others who are detained in captivity, and by the story of very many, that if the Legate had not been hindered by the opposition of those of whom we made mention above but, as he had ordered, had advanced against the Sultan before or after the swelling of the river, then Egypt would have fallen to the lot of the Christians. For at that time the leaders of Egypt were disagreeing with the Sultan; and like Rahab the harlot, begging the kindness of God for her people, for herself, and for her house,[6] so the Egyptians sent presents and gifts to our captives in Cairo, begging that by means of them, they might find mercy at the hands of the victorious Christians. On the third day of the octave of the apostles [July 6], the Legate, beginning with a three days' fast, and assembling the

[2] Ludwig of Wittelsbach, Duke of Bavaria, Count Palatine of the Rhine 1214–31. He took the Cross with Frederick in 1215.

[3] Ulrich of Andechs-Diessen, Bishop of Passau since 1215, who died on the journey homeward on October 30, 1221. He had taken the Cross with Duke Ludwig of Bavaria in 1215.

[4] Herman V, Marquis of Baden, brother of Henry I of Baden, 1212–31. Herman was back home by March 1222, and died in 1243.

[5] According to Röhricht, *Regesta regni Hieros.*, p. 250, this is Walter IV of Brienne, nephew of King John of Jerusalem. He married Marie of Cyprus, daughter of King Hugh I, became Count of Jaffa, and was killed fighting the Saracens in 1241.

[6] *See* Josue 2.

clergy with the archbishops and bishops, carried barefoot the saving banner of the Cross in procession beyond Damietta to the camp located where the river rises. On the next day King John returned to Damietta, bringing a numerous following.

CHAPTER 55

"I will begin and I will make an end," saith the Lord. "Behold I shall make a word, and whosoever shall hear it both his ears shall tingle." [1] Mine is the dominion in the kingdoms of men, "My counsel shall stand, and all My will shall be done; there is no one who can resist My countenance. There is no wisdom, there is no prudence, there is no counsel against the disposition of My will. For the whole world before Me is as the least grain of the balance, and as a drop of the morning dew that falleth down upon the earth. Who shall say to Me, 'what hast Thou done?' or who shall withstand My judgment? I have found David My servant, with My holy oil I have anointed him" [2] king of the Indies, whom I have commanded to avenge My wrongs,[3] to rise against the many-headed beast, to whom I have given victory over the king of the Persians; I have placed a great part of Asia under his feet. The King of the Persians, being lifted up unto excessive pride, wished to be the monarch of Asia; against him King David,[4] who they say is the son of Prester John, won the first fruits of victory. Then he subjugated other kings and kingdoms to himself, and, as we learned by a report that reached far and wide, there is no power on earth that can resist him. He is believed to be the executor of divine vengeance, the hammer of Asia.

[1] I Kings 3:11–12.
[2] Isaias 46:10; Jeremias 49:19; Proverbs 21:30; Wisdom 11:23; 12:12; Psalms 88:21.
[3] Probably a reference to Daniel 7.
[4] *See* p. 50, n. 2. Oliver states that King David was considered the son of Prester John. As mentioned in the note cited, others considered him to be John's nephew. This presumably refers to Jenghiz Khan's conquest of the Shah of Khwaresm, who could properly be called King of Persia.

CHAPTER 56

Indeed after the capture of Damietta, the Legate of the Apostolic See had a book which was written in Arabic read aloud briefly and by means of an interpreter, in the hearing of the multitude; and as we considered and contemplated the antiquity of its bindings and maps, we discovered we ought to proceed. This book is entitled "The Book of Clement,"[1] written, as they say, from the lips of the Prince of the Apostles by Clement himself concerning the revelations made known to Peter by the Lord between His resurrection and ascension. Now this book begins from the creation of the world and ends in the consummation of time; and in it are read the precepts and counsels of salvation. He inserts prophecies, certain of which now clearly appear to have been completed, though some depend upon the future. Among other things, it is said that a watery city would be captured by the Christians along with one city of Egypt. The capture of Alexandria is also added, nor is Damascus omitted, which greatly tortured and is still torturing the servants of God. Besides, mention is made of two kings, one of whom, it is claimed, will come from the East, the other from the West, to Jerusalem in that year when Easter will be on the third of April. This book agrees in many things with the one of which we made mention above. Very many letters written about the victory of King David support this prophecy, along with the story well-known among Christians and Saracens. We also see as a proof of this that the Christian captives of this king were freed by messengers of King David in Baghdad; these had been taken in the siege of Damietta, and the King of Babylon had sent them to the Caliph as a gift.

CHAPTER 57

On July 17th, the Christian army gathered at Fareskur, a casale three miles distant from Damietta,[1] and being suitably drawn up in

---
[1] Jacques de Vitry gives the correct title as *Revelationes beati Petri apostoli a discipulo eius Clemente in uno volumine redactae.*

[1] South of Damietta.

THE CAPTURE OF DAMIETTA

ranks of horsemen and troops of foot soldiers, they went forward quickly. Indeed estimators of the army enumerated twelve hundred men armed in military fashion, provided with the cavalry equipment necessary to accomplish such an undertaking, not counting the Turcopoles [2] and numerous other horsemen. We could not find out the exact count of armed foot soldiers because of their great number; the Saracens compared them to locusts because they occupied a great amount of land. We believe that four thousand archers assembled, almost twenty-five hundred of whom were mercenaries. Among the six hundred and thirty larger and smaller ships we clearly counted three hundred casques with eighteen armed galleys, and besides, there were scalanders, tartans,[3] barbots, corsairs, and barks carrying cargoes with provisions. The number of the enemy was declared by fugitives to have been about seven thousand horsemen. The arrangement of the battle line was as follows:

The river on the right, covered over with ships, afforded protection in the manner of a wall; on the left side, the foot soldiers served as a breastwork, going forward in line and in a procession, as it were, in close formation. The lines of horsemen were stretched out diagonally from the river to the ranks of the foot soldiers, giving them support and receiving it from them. The lancers stayed constantly with the archers, sustaining the attack of the enemy with lances close-packed and leveled, if at any time they presumed to rush into close combat. Thus in the danger of horses and horsemen it was provided by prudent counsel that the pack animals should not be wounded. The common people, unarmed, proceeded in safety with their bundles at the bank of the river; clerics, foot soldiers, and women carried water to those farther off; those who were more experienced against the snares of the deceitful, cautiously sustained the attacks of the enemy in the fore and rear guard. By public edict severe precaution was taken that no one should presume to go ahead of the foremost ranks or to fall behind the rear line or to break into the line in any wise. The scouts of the

[2] Natives of mixed origin who fought on horseback in native fashion. They were usually light cavalry or mounted archers, and are found in all the eastern armies from Byzantium to Cairo.

[3] A small one-masted vessel with a large lateen sail and a foresail.

enemy regarding our forces from both sides of the river and marveling at the order of our military discipline, tried in vain to inflict losses; but such a great multitude of archers resisted them that we learned that on that day none of our men had been captured and none of our men had been wounded, who had stayed constantly with the four-sided battle line. The Legate distributed wages with a generous hand to the knights and their attendants, he armed ships, sparing neither his body nor his possessions to accomplish the work, exhibiting all the diligence he could; in company with him King John of Jerusalem and the Duke of Bavaria, the archbishops and bishops, and the masters of the Houses toiled and labored at the undertaking.

CHAPTER 58

On July 19th the king of Egypt sent a stronger and greater proof of the might which he then had—four thousand horsemen, it seemed, who encircling the people of God timidly enough from without, at a distance, attacked the outermost lines of foot soldiers with arrows. Our men valiantly resisted them, not breaking their own lines in the least on account of this. On the following day, they besieged us more fiercely and compelled our men to use up quite a few arrows. In these two days the few Christians slightly wounded, and the very few dead, took away from the enemy the hope of winning a victory. Returning to their lord on the third day, they opened a peaceful way for us through Saramsah,[1] burning their casalia before us. Nevertheless we found plenty of grain and barley and vegetables, even straw, and the fruits of gardens; the inhabitants with their women and children fled altogether before the face of the power of God.

CHAPTER 59

On the vigil of Saint James [July 24] we pitched camp on a triangular head of an island where the Nile divides in two parts, and separates the former camp of the Sultan from ours, and where he

[1] Saramsah, a casale near the Nile, where the Sultan had a palace, described in the next chapter.

had made a delay after the capture of Damietta. In this spot the river of Tanis, withdrawing from the bed which goes to Damietta, forms with it an island. This island, extending twelve miles in length, contains many casalia located above the waters. Among those on the farther shore better known than the others and more wealthy, are Symon and Saramsah, in which there were the magnificent palaces of the king. This island has obtained a name, and is called the land of Damietta; the one which is across the river is called the land of Tanis, but the wider one which is found across the river of Damietta is called Mahalech. Beyond the river of Tanis, less than one day's journey to the east, begins the solitude of the desert, in which, however, water is found at fixed watering places, sufficient for men and animals, if it is increased by digging. Now it ends at Darum and Gaza.[1] Babylon, being located in the south, causes the land of Egypt to be called Babylonia. The plan of this city, divided into three parts, forms a triangle. The city of Babylon itself, built upon the Nile, is extensive in its length and width, having narrow streets and dwellings crowded together because of the great number of people. In it there are very many churches of the Christians, and a numerous multitude of these same people serve the prince of the land under tribute. In it are set down the wares of traders coming from Leemannia,[2] Ethiopia, Libya, Persia, and other regions. From the side opposite Damietta at a distance of almost a mile, Cairo spreads out in buildings and spacious streets; it has magnificent mansions, in which the barons of the land and the nobler citizens stay. This city does not descend entirely to the river as does Babylon, but a space planted with rush-like roots is found between. At a distance a rather high watchtower, the royal fort, stands out, plain to see, and well protected by great towers. The great buildings are arranged in a threefold way after the manner of a triangle. Now from both sides of the fort the wall comes down, enclosing Cairo and Babylon, but a sandy stretch lies between these three buildings, in which a numerous army can remain.

[1] Darum and Gaza are on the southwestern coast of Palestine and marked the border between Palestine and Egypt.
[2] According to Hoogeweg, p. 262, n. 1, this name is found nowhere else. Oliver seems to apply it to that part of Egypt which lay directly north of Ethiopia. (*See* Chapters 61 and 62.)

CHAPTER 60

Between Cairo and Babylon they point out the Church of Blessed Mary where she is said to have made a pause with the Child Jesus, when she fled into Egypt and the idols of Egypt fell. Cairo is a three days' journey distant from Damietta. From Cairo to the garden of balsam, there is a distance of a mile; this garden, which has sandy soil, is enclosed by a wall. There is a fountain in the middle and from it is derived a tale of the ancient people which is spread abroad by a famous story, that the glorious Virgin drew it forth by her prayer, and washed the clothing of the Infant Savior in it. Now this garden is cultivated in the manner of vineyards. A trunk of this garden has the thickness of a plant; its branches shoot out from the trunk to the height of one cubit in the manner of a willow, and its bark is knotty and lined, and of a whitish color. Its wood is called sirobalsam, its seed, carpobalsam, its sparse and pointed leaf, like the leaf of the licorice, is called filobalsam, and also opobalsam in whose branches the farmers make cuts in certain parts of the bark where the balsam is drawn forth, so that the liquid, collecting by degrees, may run out through them. In autumn the balsam is collected in this way: A branch is twisted and scratched with a nail; through this small opening a drop is caught and kept in dishes; next it is melted for twenty days in the sun, and afterwards is skimmed off at the fire; the fluid is poured off into bottles, for of the original substance, very little unmixed balsam remains after the purification. But the sellers and resellers usually mix in pine resin or turpentine and deceive the buyers, and therefore it is rarely found pure at the hands of venders. The Sultan usually distributed it in bottles among the princes of the earth as a great gift. The master of this garden is a Christian, having Christian and Saracen servants under him.

CHAPTER 61

Below Cairo an island extends for a stretch of three miles in length and width, where the Nile divides its waters into two parts, touching the bank of Damietta on one side, and of Rosetta on the other. Rosetta was a great city, now in ruins, between Alexandria and Damietta, but much closer to Alexandria, and two days away from Cairo. At Rosetta and above it, the river is wider, the water deeper, the harbor calmer than at Damietta; for it receives heavily laden ships, and it is possible to place a large army on the aforesaid island. When we were at its head in the siege of Damietta, the Sultan wished to take the river from us; having tried often but in vain to cause its waters to flow into a channel; after great expense he left its course to nature. From Babylon on the upper side to Leemannia, the culture of the land is hedged in by both sides of the river, having vast solitudes on both sides. Leemannia abounds in a variety of spices which she sends out and which various traders of the kingdom carry away.

CHAPTER 62

Beyond Leemannia, Ethiopia holds very broad lands, and has an innumerable Christian population partly under Christian kings and partly under the rule of the Saracens. Here are the Nubians who are joined in the Sacrament of the Altar, and in other Jacobite divine offices,[1] with this exception: The Nubians are the only ones who imprint upon their little ones with heated iron a threefold character of the Cross on the forehead near the eyes on both sides. Nevertheless they do baptize. The former and the latter have the Chaldean writing; they use leavened bread for the Holy Eucharist; they make the sign of the Cross with one finger; they say that two natures are united in the one nature of Christ, perhaps using equivocally the name of nature, so that in the second place they take "nature" for "person." [2]

---

[1] Jacobite is the usual name for the native Monophysite Christians (*see* n. 2, below) of Syria and Mesopotamia, named after James (Jacobus) el-Baradai by whom they were organized in the 6th century. They admit only the first three oecumenical councils, and claim that consecration in the liturgy is performed by the epiclesis—a prayer to send down the Holy Spirit on the bread and wine at Mass.

[2] Monophysitism is the name given to the heresy that there is only one nature in Christ, His humanity being entirely absorbed in His divinity, and His body not of one substance with ours. It was an extreme reaction from Nesto-

CHAPTER 63

The Georgians [1] and the Greeks agree in everything pertaining to divine services, but the Georgians have their own writing. While we were carefully examining their books on the mountain of Saint Simeon on the Pillar, where they have their own church, we learned through an interpreter that they have the same order of Gospels that the Latins have, and the canons of the Gospels on arcuated columns as we do. The order of the Epistles of Saint Paul is exactly the same with them as it is with us; they put the Epistle of Saint Paul to the Romans before all the others.

CHAPTER 64

The Maronites [1] have their patriarchate on the side of Mount Lebanon. These received the plan of their ecclesiastical rites from Pope Innocent in the last Lateran Council, and they observe it insofar as their writing allows, which is Chaldean, or near-Chaldean. To these people on the side of the same mountain are joined the Neophorites [2] who keep their law concealed. They do not explain

---

rianism (see p. 80, n. 1), which stated that in Christ there were two persons joined together. Monophysitism was brought into wide discussion by Eutyches (448), but its chief defender was Dioscorus, Patriarch of Alexandria. It was officially condemned by the Council of Chalcedon (451) but never died out.

---

[1] The Georgians formed an independent unit of the Orthodox Eastern Church. They were established in the 4th century, and entered into schism in the 13th.

---

[1] A nation and church of Arabic-speaking Syrians who live chiefly in the Lebanon. Their name comes from St. Maron, a Syrian abbot who died in 433. They seem to have professed a heresy known as Monothelitism from the 7th century till 1182. Their union with Rome at that time is one of the few lasting results of the crusades.

[2] Possibly the Neophorites are the same as the Druzes, a people of Asiatic Turkey and of Syria between Damascus to the east and Saida to the south. Their origin is full of fables, but they probably came from an Egyptian Mohammedan sect founded by the Caliph of Egypt, Hakim Biamrillah (996–1020), who founded a new sect of Ismalian Shiites. The Druzes now number about 200,000, and proved very bad neighbors to the Maronites in the 19th century.

it to their sons and grandsons until the thirtieth year of their age. It is an evil law that desires to be kept secret and not to appear in the light. When we wished to know, as we were passing through that section, why they never revealed their law to their wives or daughters or sisters except at this age, one of the older men answered that women were made by the devil. And we responded, "When you embrace women of this kind, do you therefore embrace the devil?" Whereupon he withdrew from us confused. Certainly the Christians are sorry that they have such neighbors.

CHAPTER 65

The Armenians [1] have their own writing. In the field their priests set aside the grain from which they wish to make unleavened hosts; they thresh it separately from the common crop; they grind it separately and on the day when they wish to consecrate the Body of the Lord, with the singing of psalms before the altar they prepare the flour and sprinkle it with water for the Paschal bread, which is in the shape of the Latins. They celebrate with great devotion. However, they are very much to blame in this, that they do not celebrate the Nativity of the Lord with us; [2] they plough and sow on that day while their women spin and card wool. They call the day of the Epiphany "baptisterium"; on this solemnity they assemble with a great crowd of people. They celebrate the Nativity of the Lord with the Epiphany, saying that the Lord was born on the same day as that on which He was baptized after a few years had elapsed. They say that they are subject to Roman laws and they have a catholicos as primate whom they obey in all things.

[1] The Armenian church dates back to at least the 3rd century and the work of St. Gregory the Illuminator. The Synod of Dovin in 527 adopted Monophysitism. Since that time the Armenian church has been the most national and the most isolated in Christendom. Reunion with Rome was proclaimed in 1198, but was never fully attained and failed completely in 1375. The rite still reveals much Latin influence.

[2] The Armenians are the only sect in the world who keep Christmas and Epiphany (January 6) as one feast.

CHAPTER 66

Stopping at Antioch, we carefully examined the Nestorians,[1] who have their church there, and who say that they believe that two natures are united in the person of Christ. They confess that the Blessed Virgin is the mother of God and of man, and that she bore both God and man, which Nestorius denied. But whether they believe in their hearts as they confess in their lips, God knows.

CHAPTER 67

The Syrians have the Greek writing, chant, and ritual sacrifice, but the Arabic language in common with the Saracens in the deeds and letters which they draw up.

CHAPTER 68

The Jacobites for the most part throughout Egypt are circumcised, but those who remain among the Medes and Persians are content with baptism.[1]

CHAPTER 69

The Russi have their own language, but in divine services they are found to be like the Greeks in everything. These different kinds of Christians are mingled with the Saracens throughout all Asia, and so that perfidious nation cannot excuse herself on the ground of ignorance.

---

[1] Nestorius, Bishop of Constantinople, who died *ca.* 451, stated that in Christ two persons were joined together, namely, God the Son and the man Jesus, Who alone was born of the Blessed Mother, and Who alone died on the Cross. Nestorius' teachings were anathematized by the Council of Ephesus (431), and his followers fled to Persia. They once formed a mighty, but now small, Nestorian church.

[1] The Egyptian Monophysites are not Jacobites, but Copts. Oliver here uses an incorrect nomenclature for them.

CHAPTER 70

We have made this long digression not without reason, so that the location of Egypt and the course of the river as well as the variety of Christian inhabitants who are in Asia may appear more clearly to the faithful. Now, as we return to the order of our history, let us sprinkle this book with tears, weeping and grieving for the loss and disgrace of Christianity.

An advance to the great and famous casale of Saramsah, of which we made mention above, was of advantage to the army of Christ. Therefore, after the capture of Damietta, the Sultan, prudently looking out for what could happen in the future, destroyed the casale as well as his beautiful palace located on the Nile. Beyond that spot the river curves and turns back and a certain little stream, coming from the island of Mahalech, flows into it; taking on depth from the waters which increase as they spread out, it is able to bear galleys and other vessels of moderate size. When our leaders saw it, they scorned it and passed it by, hastening to the head of the island. The people also, in hopes of plunder, because it was falsely announced to them that the Sultan was preparing for flight, hurried eagerly like birds to a snare, and fishes to a net. But when the King of Babylon was informed that Saramsah had been abandoned from the rear, he united foot soldiers and horsemen from his own kingdom, from Cairo and Alexandria particularly, in an attack on those who were arriving. Whereupon, our captives, considering the fact that Cairo had been evacuated by its inhabitants, formed a plan to seize the towers at our arrival, and to open them to those who were approaching. But a divine Providence which mercifully "heard the groans of them that were in fetters," [1] and the labors and sorrows of those who were in bondage, released them through our distress.

[1] Psalms 101:21.

CHAPTER 71

While this was taking place in Egypt, Seraphus, King of Edessa,[1] the city of the Medes, with Coradin, Lord of Damascus, and the leaders of Hamah[2] and Homs,[3] with a great multitude of horsemen, gathered from all regions of the east, and assembled at Homs. As a result great fear struck the people of Antioch and Acre, and other cities on the coast whose warriors were absent since they had set out on an expedition. Those in Safita, in the country of Tripoli, were especially concerned about this assemblage.

Long and earnestly did the forenamed princes deliberate whether they should come to the aid of Egypt themselves, or whether they should divide the army of the Christians by besieging some one of their fortresses. The power of King David influenced them, since as victor over the king of the Persians in the lands of the Persians and in those of Baghdad, he was acting powerfully, and on account of him they were afraid to go far from their own lands. They also reflected that the castles of the Hospitallers or the Templars could not easily be captured in a short time. Finally the counsel of those who urged advance into Egypt prevailed, especially because their brother frequently sent messengers on courier camels begging them to come. He added that the Christians had taken up their position in such a place that they could not leave it without danger, or that if they could not prevail against them when they came, they would at least arrange peace with them. The Queen of Cyprus wrote to the Legate, and the brothers of the Hospital and of the Temple wrote to their masters about these troops and their plan, urging them not to retreat from Damietta; or, if they had gone out, to look out for themselves in safe places. But now just when the sins of us all needed it, sane counsel was far removed from our leaders; like Julius Caesar,[4] repeatedly forewarned, and like Alexander the Macedonian,[5] warned in the si-

---

[1] See p. 69, n. 10. He was called King of Aleppo previously.

[2] The classical Epiphania, on the Orontes in Syria. It belonged to an Ayyubid house, descended from Taki ed din, a nephew of Saladin.

[3] In Syria, about 90 miles north-northeast of Damascus.

[4] See Suetonius, *De Vita Caesarum*, I, 83.

[5] See Curtius Rufus, *Historiae Alexandri Magni*, X, 4.

lence of the night, they neglected to employ precautions against physical danger. The Lord Himself spoke through Moses to the sons of Israel: "Go not up nor fight, for I am not with you, lest you fall before your enemies." [6] They went up, none the less, and they fell conquered. But King John, reflecting more deeply on the matter, wisely showed that the proposal so often proffered by the enemy ought to be accepted, rather than that the people of the faithful, being led forth on a longer march, should be exposed to chance accidents. But the Supreme Pontiff forbade any agreement without a special degree of the Roman Church; the Emperor, through letters sealed with gold, would not permit peace or a treaty to be arranged with the Saracens.[7]

CHAPTER 72

Meanwhile we strengthened our fort by a deep ditch; on the other hand our adversaries made a wall of earth and high bulwarks on the opposite banks of both rivers, setting up on them machines, petraries, and ballistae with a lathe, causing serious injury to the men and to the animals who were taken out to drink. The strength of our adversaries increased daily; our gathering, being depleted, proved unfaithful. As the time for passage drew near, timidity increased among those who, going away openly or deceitfully, deserted us in the camp. Many ships also, that went to Damietta to bring food, could not return. For on the 18th day of August four of our galleys were captured or sunk in the river; this gave added courage to the enemy. For the Sultan had sunk some of his galleys all through the river, of which we made mention above, below our camp through the island of Mahalech at the bank of the river, without our knowledge; this cut off passage for our men, so that

[6] Numbers 14:42.
[7] Pelagius had been instructed to communicate any proposed terms to the Pope. When Honorius learned the terms of Al-Kamil, he replied that he regretted the loss of life, the labor, and the expense entailed in refusing them, but that Frederick's recent assurance that he would sail to the East made him decide against accepting them. Honorius was influenced also by the reports concerning "Prester John" and "King David" that were prevalent, reports really based on the exploits of Jenghiz Khan and his Tartars. Frederick also, in several letters, forbade that Damietta be exchanged for Jerusalem.

they could go neither up nor down. Besides, since a multitude of armed men had wisely been stationed there, a continual guard night and day watched both banks as far as Damietta, so that our people could neither send nor receive messengers.

CHAPTER 73

From the day when we lost the river our men frequently assembled to consult together, and to ponder what would be more expedient: to wait in camp for the galleys promised by the emperor, or to go out, no matter what the loss, because of our dwindling supply of food. The greater number counseled going out, which was more dangerous because of the arrival of the enemy and the decided hindrance of the waters. But a certain one of the lesser members,[1] who saw and heard these things and described them with a crude but truthful pen, proposed David as an example, who having choice among three things, any one of which was hard, chose not a famine of seven years, nor to be conquered by an enemy for three months, but what was the common wish of the king and the poor people: a pestilence of three days. Wherefore he answered, when he was consulted, as did the weak and infirm whom there were not sufficient ships nor animals to carry, that help should be awaited in a fortified place, since the provisions, if they were carefully distributed, could last even for twenty days. Nevertheless this plan was not accepted, but a departure, and that by night, was more favored. In this, the opinion of the Bishop of Passau and that of the Bavarians prevailed.

CHAPTER 74

Therefore on August 26th in the first watch of the night, when the tents were taken up, the first men, following the judgment of their own will, and not that of reason, put fire to the tents; then others also did it eagerly, as if they were announcing their own flight, and inviting the Egyptians, who had already surrendered their bodies to sleep, to follow us. At the same time the Nile had received its full

[1] Oliver himself (*see* Hoogeweg, p. 270, n. 1).

increase, and, as its waters surged even higher than usual, it had flooded the fields. The forenamed kings also came through the desert above the river Tanis at Symon, where a bridge was built, and stopped and encamped. It added greatly to our misfortune that the people were greatly intoxicated that day with wine of which there was such an abundance that it could not be brought along; but being freely exposed, it had overwhelmed the unwary, who remained sound asleep in the camp or prostrate on the road. They were unwilling to be roused, and in great part they left us, being either cut off or captured. Others came into the overflow of the river in the shadows of night, and struggling wretchedly in the deep mire, stayed behind the others. Others, falling into the ships and pressing them down too much with their weight, were drowned. On the same night we lost camels and mules carrying burdens, including the silver vessels, clothing, and tents of the rich, and what was more disastrous, the arrows of defense. The Templars, bringing up the rear at their own great risk, stayed constantly together as a protection for those who went ahead, as they were prepared with weapons. But those who went ahead, going into different roads, wandered through the darkness of the night like sheep astray. The Egyptians were informed of our flight by the fire and smoke and promptly followed after us. They reached us even more quickly and inflicted on the Christians losses which we cannot describe. No less danger and injury was sustained by those who went down in a ship along the bank. The ship of the Legate, carrying a great number of the sick, as well as provisions, was extremely well fortified with armed men and archers, just as if it were a fort, and valiantly protected the galleys which naturally stayed close together; but hurrying too much, perhaps because of the force of the current, and being fatally separated from the land army, it could not supply food to us at the proper time. Furthermore, one of our ships filled with German warriors got too far away from the Legate's ship and was surrounded on all sides by galleys of the enemy; while sinking one of them into the deep after a long defense, it caught fire and destroyed the combatants. A scalander of the Legate carrying many temporal goods, and one small galley of the Templars in which were fifty ballistae, besides other equipment of brave men, was seized and went out of our possession.

Why do I linger over the enumeration of the losses which that night caused us? "Let a darksome whirlwind seize upon that night, let it not be counted in the days of the year, nor numbered in the months. Let that night be solitary and not worthy of praise." [1] In the beginning of this night the King of Egypt, quickly sending messengers, had the sluices broken (which those people usually call "calig") through which there could be a passage for us. Their own night is memorable to the Egyptians, and to us also. When the banks had been burst to a great extent, the superabundance of water, following the declivity of the reservoirs through conduits, softened the earth, made dry by long drought, into sticky mud which held tight the horses' hoofs; it made the open space of the fields quite impassable and greatly hindered horses and riders.

CHAPTER 75

Around the first hour of the following Friday [Aug. 27] there appeared the great and fearful cavalry of the Turks harassing us at the right; annoying galleys went up and down at the left; a phalanx of Negroes going on foot and using the marshy places for a camp pressed upon us savagely from the rear; and also a wedge-shaped formation of enemies, coming from the front, denied us rest. In this contingency King John made an attack on the Turks who were opposite him, and returned to his own battle line. The Templars, with the Hospitallers of Saint John who at that time were united with them, did not tolerate the insolence of the Ethiopians. As they massacred them they made them jump onto the bank like frogs, and even drove them back when they wished to approach the bank on our side. Thus about a thousand of the great multitude, swimming away or suffering wounds, perished. On account of this misfortune our opponents retreated a little. And since we were not permitted to go forward, the king ordered a few tents, which had stayed behind, to be taken up; nevertheless, through that whole day our adversaries stayed close to us, attacking us fiercely with their archers. We put our foot soldiers against them as a rampart and used them also, for they shot back the arrows directed against

[1] Job 3:6–7.

us. Our horsemen, laboring under the constant weight of their armor, served as a protection to the foot soldiers. On the following night, whether by the command of the Sultan or without his knowledge, the Egyptians broke open the floodgates and made the waters pour in upon the heads of those who were sleeping. Before daybreak, when darkness still covered the earth, the Ethiopian foot soldiers came who had escaped the grasp of the river, desiring to avenge their losses; they swarmed like locusts, and although for the greater part they were naked, they attacked our rear lines. You could see that our knights and their attendants were attempting flight in a closely packed throng; and the common people, being unarmed, displayed manifest timidity, but being blocked on all sides by the waters and the enemy, they had nowhere to flee. However, the Marshal of the Temple with his battle line which he was leading, raised his banner, turned upon those who were pursuing, and forced them to halt and retreat.

CHAPTER 76

At this juncture, distress which gave understanding persuaded the leaders of the multitude to send messengers for terms of peace. But Imbert,[1] a worker of great evil, took with him those whom he could get away, and went over to the enemy, explaining the whole of our distress to the Sultan. This Imbert usually took part in the secret councils of the Lord Legate, and was by far the worst traitor of that time. Nevertheless, the Sultan heard the messengers patiently, and, pending a confirmation, ordered his men to cease from disturbing us. And although his brother, and especially the Lord of Homs, who was extremely hostile to the name of Christian, tried to dissuade him from an agreement, saying that since the Franks were blocked on all sides by water, they could not escape, he himself, like a wise and mild man, desired an arrangement of peace more than the shedding of blood. Therefore, he held a secret council with his brothers and the great men of his kingdom. He proposed as an example the King of the Persians, who was exceedingly

[1] The identity of this traitor Imbert is not known. Oliver seems to be the only author who mentions him.

lifted up in mind because of many events, and shook off the yoke of subjection or servitude to the King of Babylon himself and other kings of Asia. King David conquered him on the battlefield, took away Persia, and destroyed its greatest and wealthiest cities. After this, the messengers of peace spoke on both sides, as is usually done in matters of this kind, and protracted the business all through the Saturday and Sunday following, even until evening, settling upon nothing definite.

CHAPTER 77

On the very day of the Beheading of Saint John the Baptist [Aug. 29], at about the twelfth hour, our side, urged on by the lack of food and fodder, but especially by the great size of the waters, decided that it was more honorable to live happily or to die bravely in war, than to perish infamously in the flood. So when all the Franks had been roused to combat, battle lines were drawn up here and there looking upon each other fiercely and dreadfully. But the Turks realized that he who provokes an enemy is by his own fault bound by a yoke; they retreated a little upon receiving a command from their King, and the arrival of nightfall prevented a battle. Besides, while the treaty of peace was pending, a display of treachery was feared by wise men, if the common good were to be destroyed by a dangerous attack.

CHAPTER 78

And so on the 30th day of August, being forced into a lamentable peace by the perversity of circumstances, we surrendered to the Egyptians and Assyrians, that we might be filled with bread; and thus the flood of waters and the lack of food, not the bow or the sword, humbled us in the land of our enemies. An astonishing thing, an astounding thing, a thing to be handed down to the knowledge of the future: At one and the same time the just judgment of divinity appeared and the moderation of mercy shone clearly in opportune assistance. The enormity of our evil deeds and the vast number of our crimes were compelling the vengeance of divine decision, but the natural Fount of Goodness, Whose property it is always to have mercy and to spare, mitigated the sentence of just severity. For this did we fall into danger, that by the mediation of mercy, a miracle might shine forth. "God will not have His creature to perish, and recalling, intends that he that is cast off should not altogether perish." [1] The angel of great counsel, speaking for man, as one among thousands appealed for us, announcing the justice of man; [2] for although we may be sinners, nevertheless, carrying His Cross we have left homes or parents or wives or brothers or sisters or sons or fields for the sake of Him Who shows anger placidly, Who judges calmly, Who chastises lovingly, having the blows of a father, but the heart of a mother.

CHAPTER 79

And so when the conditions had been laid down according to the decisions of the Sultan, the documents of the contracts were completed by both sides, oaths were sworn, and hostages were named. The Sultan, therefore, placing his right hand on a paper which he had signed, swore in this way: "I, Kamil, King of Babylon, from a pure heart and a good will, and without interruption, do swear by the Lord, by the Lord, by the Lord and my law, that I will in good faith observe all the things that this written paper contains which is placed under my hand; if I shall not do this, may I be separated from future judgment and the society of Mohammed, and may I acknowledge the Father, the Son, and the Holy Ghost." In this manner swore Seraphus and Coradin, and their more eminent emirs. Behold under how many mistakes and contradictions is that blind nation laboring; three times they name God, but not knowing the mystery of the Trinity, they are unwilling to distinguish the name of the Father, of the Son, and of the Holy Ghost, to the increase of their own damnation. If they swear in bad faith or with

[1] II Kings 14:14.
[2] *See* Job 33:23. The Latin text as given by Hoogeweg seems in need of a slight emendation. Oliver is clearly quoting the Latin text of Job which has *unus de millibus* (one among thousands). By an easily understandable slip of the pen Oliver's text now has *unum de similibus*, which does not make very clear sense.

any interruption of the form of the ritual, they say that they are not under obligation. Now this writing contained an agreement of this kind: that they would restore the True Cross,[1] along with all captives taken any time at all in the kingdom of Babylon, or all Christians held in the power of Coradin; and that when they had received Damietta with all its belongings, they would send us all away free, as well as all our movable goods, and would faithfully keep a truce of eight years. Our leaders swore that they would free all Saracen captives, whom they were holding in the two kingdoms of Egypt and Jerusalem; that they would restore Damietta and would observe the treaty, unless our crowned King who was coming should wish to break it. Besides, twenty-four hostages were given, whom the Sultan chose: the Legate, the King of Jerusalem, the Duke of Bavaria, and three masters of Houses, along with eighteen others. On the other hand, the son of the Sultan, heir of the kingdom, and one of his brothers of whom there are many, and sons of nobles were given to us until our return to Turo [2] and the port of Damietta.

CHAPTER 80

Let all posterity know that in view of the critical point of our necessity, we made an excellent bargain, when the Wood of our redemption was restored to us in exchange for one city which Christianity could not hold for long, since grain or wheat is spoiled there in less than a year and the master of Egypt himself can scarcely keep it peopled; and when so many thousands of captives, in whose number we counted ourselves, from the greatest to the least, were restored to their own freedom. When the Emperor Heraclius entered Persia, he captured it with difficulty after five successive years; and having defeated Chosroes, he carried the Cross of the Lord in triumph and brought the patriarch Zachary back to Jerusalem with his captive people. The Sultan had been keeping as

[1] The earliest reference to the existence of the True Cross was mad by St. Cyril of Jerusalem in 347. The Empress Helena is said to have divided the Cross into three parts, sending one to the church of Jerusalem. It was this section that the Mohammedans had taken. (*See* p. 45, n. 1.)

[2] Situated near Damietta.

captive the Patriarch of Alexandria,[1] a man of great piety and perfection of morals; he sent him back to us as we were going up the Nile, released from his chains and free from the squalor of prison. The enemies of the Cross declare that they were deceived in this agreement, saying that they had regained their own city of Damietta, that they had destroyed Jerusalem, and other fortresses of this illustrious kingdom, but that the Christians had erected one impregnable fort in Palestine itself, very dangerous to them and without their consent.[2] Besides, if we had been completely destroyed, or imprisoned after losing all our possessions, and if Damietta had been lost without any recompense, the rest of the land which the worshipers of Christ hold would have wavered on the edge of certain danger. For those who had remained to guard Damietta, when they heard our adverse circumstances, left the city and fled, for the most part. Not only did they flee, but also those who had but recently arrived heard the unfavorable report and returned.[3] The Count of Malta [4] reached Damietta around the end of August with forty galleys. Pirates despoiled the Hospitallers of Saint John and the Templars of their goods, killed one noble knight and religious brother of the Temple who was defending what had been entrusted to him, and fatally wounded another brother, a Teutonic knight.

CHAPTER 81

Before the restoration of Damietta the Sultan began to carry out what he had promised. For he commanded that the Bishop-elect of Beauvais and certain other captives be released from chains and brought to their own camp. The Master of the army of the Temple and the Master of the Teutonic House [1] were sent by the

---

[1] Since 1219 this see had been occupied by Athanasius of Clermont in Auvergne.
[2] Château-Pélerin.
[3] The surrender of the city followed on September 8.
[4] Henry Pescatore, Count of Malta, had been sent by Emperor Frederick as admiral of his fleet.

---

[1] The Master of the Teutonic Knights at this time was the famous Herman von Salza, the ultimate councilor of Frederick II.

leaders to surrender the city in accordance with the pledge and assurance of their oath. This was done without great difficulty. For among the new pilgrims who were arriving, there was not to be found a man powerful, vigorous, and constant enough to be either willing or able to hold it after the forementioned happenings.

CHAPTER 82

"The beast has gone into his covert, and abides in his den." [1] If it is asked why Damietta returned so quickly to the unbelievers, the reason is clear: It was luxury-loving, it was ambitious, it was mutinous; besides, it was exceedingly ungrateful to God and to men. For to pass over other things, when that city had been given to us from on high by Heaven in the distribution of the riches that were found in her, not an old woman nor a boy of ten years and over was excluded; to Christ alone, the bestower of the goods, was a share denied, not even a tenth being paid to Him. Formerly Roman pagans dedicated a golden vessel to Apollo under the form of tithes; the sons of Israel according to custom assigned to the Lord His share of the spoils of the enemy; the sons of Israel said to Moses when they had conquered the Madianites, "We offer as gifts to the Lord what gold we could find in the booty, in garters, rings, tablets, bracelets, and chains." [2]

In the distribution of towers and dwellings most praise was deservedly given to that obedient and energetic nation,[3] who from the beginning attacked Damietta with great courage, and considered no position either humble or lowly; by the fleet of ships which it brought, the camp of the faithful was supplied with food and weapons, the tower of the river was captured, the crossing to the opposite bank was organized, the upper and lower bridges were built, the watchtower of Turo was constructed, the walls of the rampart were fortified. It has consolation in the face of such ingratitude since "God will render the inestimable reward" of His slaves "and will conduct them in a wonderful way." [4]

[1] Job 37:8.
[2] Numbers 31:50.
[3] The Frisians.
[4] Wisdom 10:17.

CHAPTER 83

O lover of men, King of glory, Savior of the world, Who hast holy knowledge and omnipotence above all power, Who dost reprove some and dost console others, Thou didst humble our pride by taking away Damietta from the ungrateful and by mercifully preserving Armenia and Antioch against the efforts of wicked men. For those who were in the fortress inflicted great disaster upon Christianity, but those who were then in the valley added irreverence to wickedness; as they presumptuously gathered in defiance of Thy goodness, from one side Thy justice appeared plainly, and from another the mercy of Thy customary goodness clearly shone on those who were willing to open their eyes.

CHAPTER 84

Rupen, formerly Lord of Antioch, was of very noble stock, but because of a lack of discretion he was unsuitable for the management of great things; with the help of Guérin, Master of the Hospital of Saint John,[1] and of those whom he could persuade, he seized Tarsus, attacking the Armenians because of a desire for a kingdom. This did not escape the Turcomans of Iconium. They were encouraged by the discord of the Christians, and attacked Armenia with troops. But as the leaders of that kingdom, in making their complaint, affirm and state on peril of their lives, the army of Christians in that region at that time was reduced to about twenty thousand after they counted those who had been killed or captured by the Saracens, and also after many had fled because of the loss of their goods.

[1] Guérin of Montagu, a Frenchman from the province of Auvergne, brother of Eustorgius, Archbishop of Nicosia and Peter, Master of the Temple. He was acting as Marshal of the Hospitallers when he was promoted to be Grand Master in 1208. He distinguished himself at the siege of Damietta. He had assisted at the coronation of John of Brienne in 1210, and had attended the Parliament of Acre in 1217. He died in 1228, and was succeeded by Bernard of Texis.

CHAPTER 85

Therefore in addition to all Thy praise, insofar as I am able and as Thou wilt permit, I shall continue by adding the following things.

CHAPTER 86

In the year of grace 1222 in the month of May it happened that there was a great earthquake on Cyprus, in Limasol, Nicosia, and other places of that island, especially in Paphos, to such a degree that the city was completely destroyed along with the fort; human beings of both sexes who were there at the time of the earthquake were completely lost; the harbor was dried up, where afterwards waters or fountains burst forth.

CHAPTER 87

In the month of June in that same year Coradin assembled a numerous army from Arabia, Palestine, Idumea, and Syria—ten thousand horsemen, and fifteen thousand foot soldiers—against Guy of Gibelet who, like a vain and wicked man, did not wish to take part in the general truce, nor to return the captive Saracens whom he held. Although he was well enough fortified by the difficult nature of the region and by the help of Christians, nevertheless he submitted to a truce with Coradin that was injurious to him and shameful to the Christian name.[1]

CHAPTER 88

In the month of June in the same year, the boy Philip,[1] son of Bohemond, Prince of Antioch, became a knight in Armenia; he married the daughter of Leo, formerly King of Armenia, and was

[1] Border warfare was rather usual in the north of the kingdom, even after the peace had been made. On this occasion, Guy simply refused to recognize the truce, and was compelled by Al-Moadden to a separate truce.

[1] See p. 63, n. 4.

solemnly crowned with her as King of that kingdom. And when the nuptials were being celebrated, and the Armenians were joyfully assembled for the great affair, Turks from Iconium savagely attacked that land with a great multitude, massacring whomever they could find and taking away much plunder with them. At the same time Bohemond, Prince of Antioch and Count of Tripoli, was present. Although he had only a few Latins with him at the time, since he had not foreseen this mishap, nevertheless, with his son the king he promptly and vigorously pursued the enemy over long, hard roads. Although many of his number were killed, like a vigorous man, and one skilled in arms, he drove them out beyond the boundaries of Armenia. After this, the Armenians recovered a certain well fortified camp, Siblia [2] by name, located at the boundaries of Armenia and Turkey, which the Sultan of Iconium had taken away from them along with other fortresses after the death of Leo.

CHAPTER 89

Meanwhile Frederick, Emperor of the Romans and King of Sicily, sent four galleys to Acre, summoning the King, the Patriarch, and the Master of the Hospital of Saint John. They crossed in the month of September, hastening to the Council of Verona, which had been proclaimed by the Supreme Pontiff and the Emperor for the feast of Saint Martin [Nov. 11]. At the same time, along with the forementioned princes, came Lord Pelagius, Bishop of Albano, a Legate of the Apostolic See. The Master of the Temple, with the army of the same House, remained in the land of promise for the protection of Christianity, according to the common advice of the barons, after sending discreet and honorable messengers to the Council.

[2] Identified as Sandakli in Phrygia by Röhricht (*Beiträge,* II, 197, n. 105).

Appendix A[1]

CONCLUDING SECTION OF THE DARMSTADT MANUSCRIPT

WHEN this had been so accomplished, our pilgrims grew sluggish through idleness and riotous living, and, being eager for earthly gain, they provoked the wrath of the Almighty against themselves. When He saw that we were ungrateful for the blessings we had received He judged us unworthy to receive more. Truly, since neither power nor triumph is long-lived without God on account of our sins, which in their different uncleannesses had offended the Author of our salvation, certain sons of Belial, under a false pledge of Christian faith, deceitfully suggested to us that we set out against the Sultan with all the force of our army which had been stationed in nearby forts with a multitude of pagans as great as the sands of the sea which cannot be numbered. But, hoping that the affair would be accomplished by the Lord our God, in accordance with the common advice of the pilgrims, we set out against the enemies of the faith, unwisely leaving Damietta without defense. When the Sultan, after three days, saw the flight of the pilgrims, he pretended flight on his own part, and deceitfully left his camp to be plundered by us. With the whole strength of Egypt he hurried swiftly to Damietta by another road, and established his camp in a narrow spot below the city and us, so that we could have neither retreat nor intercourse with it. Behold how sudden a change of the right hand of the Most High! Then, with God favorable to us, we reigned mightily in the land of Egypt; now, with Him against us, we drift wretchedly between Scylla and Charybdis, between hunger and thirst. For this is that day of which it is written: "That day is a day of wrath," [2] etc. Sorrow and groaning and the

---

[1] In the Darmstadt manuscript of the present work, Chapter 53 is followed by this concluding section, which was probably written by another hand.

[2] Sophonias, 1:15.

moisture of tears do not permit me to describe our tribulations and distresses, and the particular dangers of death. But since nothing was left for us but a wretched death, we all with one voice cried out to heaven to Our Lord Jesus Christ humbly begging pardon. But He Who says in His kindness, "I desire not the death of the wicked but rather that he be converted and live," [3] frequently, when He is angry, is mindful of His mercy and is also just and merciful. Since He now saw that we had been sufficiently purified by penance and a fountain of tears, He mitigated the cruelty of our enemies to such an extent that they sent messengers to us, who were wasting away with hunger, to treat of peace and concord with us, on these terms: That the Sultan might take back his city to be possessed in peace, and that he would give us safe conduct to it along with complete integrity of our persons and belongings by supplying adequate ships and provisions. But we knew that the delegation had been procured by God, since there was nothing else left for us but death or the everlasting disgrace of slavery; and we willingly embraced it, humbly returning deserved thanks to God. When these agreements had been firmly settled through hostages and oaths, the Sultan was moved by such compassion toward us that for many days he freely revived and refreshed our whole multitude. Finally when our affair had been disposed and settled, he procured ships and provisions for a just price, along with safe conduct. Who could doubt that such kindness, mildness, and mercy proceeded from God? Those whose parents, sons, and daughters, brothers and sisters we killed with various tortures, whose property scattered or whom we cast naked from their dwellings, refreshed us with their own food as we were dying of hunger, although we were in their dominion and power. And so with great sorrow and mourning we left the port of Damietta, and according to our different nations, we separated to our everlasting disgrace.

[3] Ezechiel, 33:11.

Appendix B

BRIEF LINGUISTIC COMMENTARY

FROM a linguistic viewpoint the *Historia Damiatina* contains many examples of usages in both syntax and orthography that differ from those of classical writers.

Differences in spelling occur as follows:

1. æ is found as *e* in *edificare, herere, letari, precessere, hec, que, preterea, vivifice.*

2. œ is found as *e* in *cepisse, fetor, menia, pena.*

3. *mn* occurs as *mpn* in *alumpna, columpna, dampna, sollempnitas.*

4. *h* is sometimes placed at or near the beginning of a word as in *habundantia, habundare, Jhesum.*

5. *c* is put before *h* in *nichil, nichilominus.*

6. *ci* and *ti* before vowels occur in *nunciare, pacienter, precio, delitiis.*

7. *ewangelium, obprobrium, promunctorium* appear as isolated peculiarities.

8. *apostota, barbota, Christicola, guerra, tharida, treuga, werra, girum, petrarium, scalandrus, trabuculum, cogo, manutenere, martirizo, linealiter, processionaliter, salutifere, transversaliter,* and many others are words found only in late Latin.

In the *Historia Damiatina* Oliver shows the following syntactical deviations from classical usage:

1. Abstract nouns are used, either alone or with *esse* or *facere*, to express an idea for which classical writers would have used a single verb. (Chapter 8, *essent in obsidione;* 13, *concurrerent ad ignis suffocationem;* 22, *navium immersiones fecit;* 36, *werram habens cum Sarracenis;* 43, *causas pretendens ad excusationem sui;* 76, *ab infestatione nostra;* 76, *ante restitutionem Damiate.*)

2. The genitive of the names of months in dates is employed where in classical Latin the names of months were most frequently used adjectivally in agreement with nouns. (Chapter 27, *In Ka-*

APPENDIX B 99

lendis Maii; 74, *VII Kalendas Septembris;* 32, *Nonis Novembris.*)

3. *Medius* with the genitive appears where in classical prose we would find *medius* used adjectivally. (Chapter 11, *in medio fluminis.*)

4. The ablative to express duration of time appears instead of the accusative. (Chapter 6, *Toto fere tempore;* 8, *brevi tempore commorati.*)

5. *Aliquis* is used after *ne* when no emphasis is intended. (Chapter 31, *ne aliquis nunciaret.*)

6. *Alius* is used where classical writers would employ *alter.* (Chapter 8, *pars . . . hiemavit, pars alia obsedit;* 56, *duobus regibus quorum unus . . . alius;* 83, *ab una parte . . . ab alia.*)

7. *Ad* is used with the names of cities or towns to express limit of motion. (Chapter 52, *ad Damiatam.*)

8. *Absque* appears to denote defect in reality where *sine* would appear in classical Latin. (Chapter 11, *absque scale suspensione;* 71, *absque periculo;* 81, *absque magna difficultate.*)

9. The infinitive of purpose appears once. (Chapter 2, *ascendit solus orare.*)

10. *Facere* is used with accusative and infinitive instead of *ut* and subjunctive. (Chapter 43, *alios descendere faciens;* 46, *extendi faciens tentoria;* 74, *rumpi fecit clausoria;* 75, *saltare fecerunt eosdem.*)

11. The use of a gerund in the ablative where a participle in the nominative would occur in classical Latin. (Chapter 13, *se prostraverunt . . . protestando;* 34, *magnificas gratiarum actiones altis vocibus resonando;* 85, *adiciendo prosequar sequentia.*)

12. *Fore* used with a future passive participle to express futurity in an indirect statement where classical Latin would use the future passive infinitive. (Chapter 28, *Damiatam . . . fore tradendam;* 35, *Damiatam . . . fore capiendam;* 56, *Civitatem . . . fore capiendam.*)

13. The present participle expresses time prior or subsequent to the main verb, while in classical Latin it expresses simultaneous action. (Prior: Chapter 40, *veniens ad sepulchrum transtulit eum in Alexandriam;* 74, *naviculas pondere suo prementes submersi sunt.*) (Subsequent: Chapter 75, *transivit ad hostes statum necessitatis exponens soldano;* 88, *Turci . . . sunt ingressi trucidantes . . . et praedam trahentes.*)

14. A *quod* clause appears instead of the accusative and infinitive in indirect discourse. (Chapter 3, *scientes quod . . . oculus*

penetrare non potest; 52, *intelligentes quod . . . vellet obsidere;* App., *sperantes quod res fieret a domino;* App., *scientes quod haec . . . procurata est.*)

15. An indicative verb introduced by *quod* is used in a substantive clause of result where classical prose would employ the subjunctive with *ut.* (Chapter 43, *Factum est quod Johannes castra fidelium reliquit.*)

BIBLIOGRAPHY

EDITION OF THE TEXT

Hoogeweg, O., *Die Schriften des Kölner Domscholasters, spätern Bischofs von Paderborn und Kardinal-Bischofs von S. Sabina Oliverus.* Tübingen, Bibliothek des Litterarischen Vereins in Stuttgart, CCII, 1894. The *Historia Damiatina* is found on pp. 159–282. It consists of several letters written by Oliver during the crusade. The other works of Oliver are published in the same volume.

PRIMARY SOURCES FOR THE FIFTH CRUSADE

Jacques de Vitry, *Historia Iherosolimitana*, in Bongars, *Gesta Dei per Francos.* Hanover, 1611. A partial translation is available in the Palestine Pilgrims Text Society Publications, XI, London, 1896. The text is based largely on Oliver for the account of the capture of Damietta, but it adds some material.

Recueil des Historiens des Croisades, Historiens Occidentaux, II. Paris, 1869. *L'Estoire d'Eracles* appears on pp. 321–52.

Röhricht, Reinhold, *Quinti Belli Sacri Scriptores Minores,* and *Testimonia Minora de Quinto Bello Sacro.* Geneva, Société de l'Orient Latin, Série Historique, II, III, 1879, 1882. These contain practically all of the primary sources for the Fifth Crusade except Oliver and Jacques de Vitry.

SECONDARY HISTORIES OF THE FIFTH CRUSADE

Grousset, René, *Histoire des Croisades et du Royaume Franc de Jérusalem*, III. Paris, Plon, 1936.

Hoogeweg, O., "Der Kreuzzug von Damietta," *Mittheilungen der Oesterreichischen Akademie*, 1887–88.

Michaud, M., *Histoire des Croisades.* 5 vols., Paris, 1813–22 (English translation by W. Robson, New York, 1853). Book XII covers the Fifth Crusade, which the author calls the

Sixth. The account, though detailed, is out of date and is no longer very useful.

Röhricht, Reinhold, *Geschichte des Königreichs Jerusalem*. Innsbruck, 1898.

———, *Studien zur Geschichte des Fünften Kreuzzuges*. Innsbruck, 1891.

There is no really good account of the Fifth Crusade in English. Short accounts are to be found in the following works:

Archer, T. A., and Kingsford, C. L., *The Crusades*. New York, 1898.
Campbell, G. A., *The Crusades*. London, Duckworth, 1935.
———, *The Knights Templar*. New York, R. M. McBride, 1938.
Conder, C. R., *The Latin Kingdom of Jerusalem*. London, 1897.
King, E. J., *The Knights Hospitallers in the Holy Land*. London, Methuen, 1931.

OTHER WORKS CONSULTED IN PREPARING THE NOTES

Bréhier, L., *L'Église et l'Orient, les Croisades*. 5th ed., Paris, Lecoffre, 1928.
Darbishire, R. S., "The Moslem Antagonist," *Moslem World*, XXVIII (1938), 258–71.
Dutripon, F. P., *Bibliorum Sacrorum Concordantiae*. 9th ed.,
Eubel, C., *Hierarchia catholica medii aevi*. 3 vols., Münster, 1898–1910.
Gams, P. B., *Series episcoporum ecclesiae catholicae*. Ratisbon, 1873–86.
Histoire Littéraire de la France, XVIII (1895).
Hubert, M. J., and LaMonte, J. L., *The Crusade of Richard Lion Heart by Ambroise*. New York, Columbia University Press (Records of Civilization), 1941.
LaMonte, J. L., "John d'Ibelin, the Old Lord of Beirut," *Byzantion*, XII (1937), 417–48.
Lane-Poole, S., *The Mohammedan Dynasties*. London, 1893.
Mas Latrie, L. de, *Trésor de Chronologie*. Paris, 1889.
Paris, n.d.
Rey, E. G., *Les Familles d'Outremer de DuCange*. Paris, 1869.
Röhricht, R., *Die Deutschen im Heiligen Lande*. Innsbruck, 1894.
———, *Beiträge zur Geschichte der Kreuzzüge*. 2 vols., Berlin, 1874–78.

———, *Regesta Regni Hierosolymitani.* Innsbruck, 1893; Additamentum, 1904.

Siedschlag, B., *English Participation in the Crusades, 1150–1220.* Menasha, Wis. (Privately Printed), 1939.

Stockvis, A. M. H. J., *Manuel d'histoire de généalogie et de chronologie.* 3 vols., Leyden, 1888–91.

INDEX

Abd Allah ibn Muhammed ibn Wazir, 21
Abraham, 50
Achan, 55
Acre, 12, 13, 14, 15, 17, 18, 19, 20, 22, 48, 58, 63, 67, 69, 82, 93, 95
Acts of Apostles, 60
Adam de Villebléon, 42
Adolph, count of Berg, 24
Agar, 50
Agarenes, 50
Agnes of Courtenay, 30
Agnes of France, 13
Agnes of Groitsch-Rochlitz, 12, 13
Ain Tubaûn, 14
'Ala-al-Dîn Kaîqubâd, 52
Al-Adil, 69
Alamut, 51
Al-Aziz, 69
Albano, cardinal-bishop of, 29, 31, 46, 95
Alberic, archbishop of Rheims, 22, 42
Alberic des Trois Fontaines, 42
Albigensians, 3, 12, 16
Alcacer del Sol, 20, 21; capture of, 21
Alcatia, 20
Aldenburg, 13
Aleppo, 36, 96
Alexander the Great, 7, 23, 58, 82
Alexandria, 58, 67, 72, 77, 78, 81; patriarch of, 91
Alfonso I, king of Portugal, 21
Alfonso III, king of Castile, 21
Al-Fula, 14
Alice of Gibelet, 68
Alice of Lusignan, 12, 68
Al-Kamil, 6, 30, 31, 83, 89
Al-Malik-al Aschraf, 52, 69
Al-Malik-al Moadden Isa, 36, 39, 53, 94
Al-Malik en Nasser Salah-ed-Dîn, 52
Amalric, 47

Ambroise, 32
Ambrosian Hymn, 27
Ananias, 60
Anatolia, 17, 69
André of Espeissis, 42
André of Nanteuil, 42
Andrew II, king of Hungary, 1, 12, 17
Andria, count of, 29
Angers, bishop of, 29, 42
Angoulême, see first names
Antioch, 53, 78, 82, 93, 94
Apocalypse, 47
Apollo, 92
Apulia, 62
Aquileia, patriarch of, 13
Arabia, 45, 94
Argyrokastron, 53
Armenia, 12, 52, 53, 61, 63, 69, 93, 94, 95
Armenian Church, 63
Armenians, 52, 78, 93, 95
Arundel, earl of, 62
Ascalon, 49
Asia, 71, 81, 89
Assassins, 51; their leader, 51; his power, 51
Assyrians, 88
Athanasius, patriarch of Alexandria, 91
Athlit, 18
Augustine, St., 17
Austria, duke of, 12, 13, 17, 22, 24, 26, 28, 38, 54
Avesnes, see first names
Aymeri de Layron, 43
Aymeri de Lusignan, 12, 63
Ayyubites, 69, 82

Babylon, 27, 34, 44, 45, 46, 47, 52, 57, 62, 64, 66, 72, 75, 76, 77, 81, 88, 89, 90

INDEX

Babylonians, 27, 28, 33, 41, 43, 57
Bacs, bishop of, 13
Baden, marquis of, 70
Baghdad, caliph of, 52, 72, 82
Baibars, 53
Baldwin I, 45
Baldwin II, 45
ballistae, 22
Bamberg, bishop of, 13
Bar, count of, 29, 30
Baradai, James el-, 77
barbots, 33
Bariz, 42
Bavaria, duke of, 70, 74, 90
Bavarians, 13, 84
Bayeux, bishop of, 13
Beatrice of Hohenstaufen, 13
Beaufort, 16
Beaumont, *see* Belmont, and first names
Beauvais, bishop-elect of, 42, 70, 91
Bedouins, 64
Bedum, apparitions at, 12
Beirut, lord of, 68
Beisan, 14
Bela III, 12
Belmont, 42, 65. *See also* Beaumont, and first names
Benedâb, 35
Berg, count of, 24
Bernard, bishop of Paderborn, 9
Bernard of Texis, 93
Bernard, St., 17
Berris, 42
Berthold, bishop of Hungary, 13
Berthold, duke of Meran, 12
Bethlehem, bishop of, 22, 31
Bethsaida, 14
Bethsan, 14
Bohemond IV, 17, 51, 53, 63, 68, 94, 95
Bonnevaux, abbot of, 3
Bordeaux, archbishop of, 29
Bouvines, 42
Bozanti, 52
Brabant, 3, 42
Bréhier, L., 1, 2
Bremen, 22
Brescia, bishop of, 61
Brienne, *see* first names

Broil, 65
Busdorf, monastery of, 9
Byzantium, 73

Caesarea, 17, 18, 19, 43, 58
Caiphas, 18
Cairo, 27, 29, 50, 70, 73, 75, 76, 81
Canticle of Canticles, 49
Capharnaum, 15
Cappadocia, 52
Carmel, Mount, 18
Carthage, Sea of, 20
Casimir, duke of Pomerania, 1
Caspian Sea, 51
Castle of the Son of God, *see* Pilgrims' Castle
Catholicos, 65
cats, 54
Chalcedon, 78
Chamberlain of France, 42
Champagne, count of, 13
Charybdis, 96
Chastel-Blanc, 53
Château-Pélerin, *see* Pilgrims' Castle
Chatillon-Neuilly, 42
Chatillon-sur-Marne, 42
Chester, earl of, 39, 42, 46
Chevaliers bannerets, 42
Chirbet Kurdâne, 14
Chosroes, 90
Clement, Book of, 72
Clement V, 17
cogones, 22
Cologne, 1, 2, 3, 8, 9, 20, 21, 22, 24, 48
Conrad, Cardinal, 9
Constance of Sicily, 69
Constantine, Constable, 52, 63
Constantinople, 12, 47; bishop of, 80
Copts, 80
Coradin, 36, 45, 55, 58, 59, 67, 68, 82, 89, 90, 94
Corinthians I, 22, 34; II, 32, 43
Courtenay, *see* first names
Crete, archbishop of, 61
Cross, *see* Holy Cross
Curtius Rufus, 7, 23
Cyprus, 66, 94; constable of, 41; king of, 1, 12, 17; Knights of, 41; queen of, 68, 82

INDEX

Damascus, 31, 45, 50, 52, 67, 72, 78, 82
Damietta, 1, 5, 6, 8, 10, 16, 22, 23, 24, 30, 33, 35, 37, 40, 41, 45, 46 (capture of by Christians), 47, 48, 49, 50, 51, 52, 53, 55, 56, 57, 58, 59, 61, 62, 65, 66, 69, 70, 72, 75, 76, 77, 81, 82, 83, 84, 90, 91, 92, 93, 96, 97
Daniel, 71
Darbishere, R. S., 37
Darius, 23
Darmstadt, manuscript of, 36
Darum, 75
David, king, 51, 71, 82, 83, 89; Tower of, 37
Dead Sea, 45
De itinere Frisonum, 20, 21
Denmark, king of, 9, 66
Descriptio Terre Sancte, 7
Destroit, 18, 67
De Vita Caesarum, 82
Diether of Katzenellenbogen, 66
Dietrich, archbishop of Trier, 20
Dioscorus, 78
Dokkum, 21
Dovin, Synod of, 79
Druzes, 78

Edessa, 69, 82
Egbert, bishop of Bamberg, 13
Egypt, 4, 20, 22, 27, 31, 44, 45, 46, 47, 52, 57, 58, 63, 64, 70, 74, 75, 76, 78, 79, 81, 82, 86, 90; "Doctors of," 6, 8, 52
Egyptians, 24, 33, 34, 35, 45, 46, 57, 70, 84, 85, 86, 87, 88
Emo, abbot of Wittewierum, 9
Emo's *Chronicon*, 20
Engelbert, bishop of Zeitz, 13
Engelbert, St., archbishop of Cologne, 24
English, 63, 65
Epernay, 3
Ephesians, 69
Ephesus, Council of, 80
Ephraim, 64
Epiphania, 82
Eracles, *see* Estoire
Erlau, bishop of, 13, 29

Ermaneksu, 52
Eschive d'Ibelin, 12
Esther, 43
l'Estoire d'Eracles, 8, 41
Ethiopia, 75, 77
Ethiopians, 86, 87
Etiennette of Milly, 68
Etschmiadzin, 63
Et-Tell, 15
Eusebius, Chronicle of, 50
Eustorgius of Montagu, 13, 67, 93
Eutyches, 78
Exodus, 30
Ezechiel, 60, 97

Faba, 14
Faenza, bishop of, 61
Fareskur, 72
Fifth Crusade, 3; joined by Oliver, 3; leaders of, 1; failure of, 9, 88, 89
Flanders, 3, 13
Flemish, 65
France, 39, 42; chamberlain of, 42
Franks, 18, 50, 62, 87, 88
Frederick II, German Emperor, 1, 10, 12, 20, 41, 49, 50, 61, 68, 69, 70, 83, 84, 90, 91, 95
Fresia, 21
Friesland, 3
Frisia, 6, 8, 9, 10
Frisians, 3, 4, 8, 10, 20, 24, 25, 26, 27, 29, 32, 33, 36, 56, 92
Fulcher of Chartres, *Historia Hierosolymitana*, 8

Gabriel, 37
Galilee, 14, 15
Gallic mercenaries, 63
Gaucher, 42
Gauls, 33
Gaza, 42, 75
Geldt, 3
Genesis, 48
Geneva, bishop of, 3
Genoa, 46
Genoese, 40
Gentile, Matteo, 62
George, count of Wied, 20
Georgian Church, 63
Georgians, 50, 51, 78

Gerard, bishop of Humana, 29
Germans, 18, 20, 24, 25, 26, 32, 36, 38, 46, 49, 56, 63, 85
Gerona, bishop of, 29
Gertrude of Hungary, 13
Gessen, 48
Gesta Crucigerorum Rhenanorum, 21
Gibelet, *see* first names
Gilboa, 14
Godolias, 57
Gregory the Illuminator, St., 79
Grenoble, bishop of, 3
Grousset, René, 4
Guérin of Montagu, 13, 68, 93
Guy of Brienne, 70
Guy of Gibelet, 70

Hakim Biamrillah, 78
Halgrin, Johann, 10
Hamah, 82
Hassan, 51
Harrin, 14, 45
Hayton, 63
Hedwig, St., 13
Helena, 90
Helmarhaus, monastery of, 2
Helvis, 42
Henry, bishop of Mantua, 29
Henry, count of Champagne, 12, 68
Henry, count of Schwerin, 9, 66
Henry, duke of Silesia-Breslau, 13
Henry, marquis of Istria, 13
Henry of Milly, 68
Henry of Uelmen, 42
Henry I of Baden, 70
Henry VI, 69
Henry Pescatore, count of Milan, 91
Heraclius, 90
Herdericus of Schilwolde, 9
Herman, marquis of Baden, 70
Herman von Salza, 91
Hervé, count of Nevers, 29, 30
Histoire Littéraire de la France, 44
Historia Damiatina, 1, 2; when written, 4; perhaps completed in Egypt, 4; style, 6, 7; language, 7, 8, 98-100
Historia de ortu Jerusalem et eius variis eventibus, 7, 8
Historia Regum Terre Sancte, written during siege of Damietta, 8; appears in later redaction in year 1222, 8; ends where *Historia Damiatina* begins, 8
Historiae Alexandri Magni, 23, 82
Hohenstaufen, 3, and *see* first names
Holland, count of, 20, 42
Holy Cross, 11, 14, 23, 26, 29, 41, 45, 55, 90
"Holy Mother," ship called, 33
Holy Sepulchre, 3, 37
Homs, 82, 87
Honorius III, 1, 10, 16, 29, 33, 75, 84, 89
Hoogeweg, O., 2, 7, 12, 29, 33, 75, 84, 89
Hospitallers, 16, 17, 22, 24, 41, 42, 43, 46, 52, 82, 87, 91, 93
Hubert, M. J., 32
Hugh of Angoulême, count of La Marche, 29
Hugh of Gibelet, 68
Hugh of Lusignan, king of Cyprus, 1, 12, 17, 70
Humana, bishop of, 29
Hungary, bishop of, 13, 29; king of, 1, 8, 12, 17

Ibelius, 68
Iconium, 52, 93, 95
Idumea, 94
Imbert, 87
Innocent III, 2, 3, 8, 12, 22, 29, 78
Isabelle of Jerusalem, 12, 68
Isaias, 11, 35, 41, 53, 54, 55, 57, 64, 71
Isauria, 52
Ishmael, 57
Islam, 51
Istria, margrave of, 13
Italians, 64; favor capture of Damietta, 40, 46
Italy, 46
Ithier of Toucy, 30
'Izz-al-Dîn Kaîkâwus, 52

Jacobite, 77, 79
Jacques de Vitry, 6, 16, 25, 48, 72
Jacques of Avesnes, 13
Jaffa, count of, 70
James, count of Andria, 29
Jebel Asha, 14
Jenghiz Khan, 50, 71, 83

INDEX

Jeremias, 43, 57, 73
Jericho, 55, 59
Jerome, St., 8, 50
Jerusalem, 1, 3, 12, 16, 17, 19, 31, 36, 37, 45, 46, 47, 48, 49, 55, 56, 59, 67, 72, 83, 90, 91, 95; king of, 4, 12, 15, 17, 22, 40, 42, 46, 49, 54, 58, 61, 90; patriarch of, 13, 14, 15, 16, 22, 41, 95
Job, 11, 30, 49, 87, 89, 92
John, Gospel of, 11
John de Veirac, bishop of Limoges, 22
John d'Ibelin, 12, 41, 68
John Lackland, 30, 39
John of Arcis, 42
John of Brienne, 4, 12, 15, 17, 22, 31, 35, 52, 61, 63, 70, 71, 74, 83, 87, 90, 93; withdraws from Christian army, 61; returns, 71
Jonas, 31
Jordan, 14, 15
Josue, 59, 70
Judas, 60
Judas Macchabeus, 28
Judges, 33
Julianne of Caesarea, 43
Julius Caesar, 7, 82

Kafr Abû Danes, 21
Kaîkhosru, 52
Kalocza, bishop of, 13
Katzenellenbogen, count of, 66
Khwaresm, 71
Kings I, 39, 71; II, 89; IV, 35, 43
Knights of Cyprus, 41
Koran, 37
Krak, 45

La Marche, count of, 29
Lamentations, 53
LaMonte, J. L., 32, 68
Landa, bishop of, 61
Laranda, 52
La Rochelle, 44
Lascaris, Theodore, 52
Las Navas de Tolosa, 12
Lateran Council (IV), 3, 8, 12, 22, 78
Lauwerzee, 20
Layron, see first names
Lebanon, 51, 78

Leemania, 75, 77
Legate, see Pelagius
Leo, king of Armenia, 52, 53, 61, 65, 94, 95
Leopold, duke of Austria, 1, 12
Letters of Oliver, 8; ten survive, two of them source for first part of *Historia Damiatina*, 8
Libya, 75
Liége, 27; Chronicle of, 42
Limasol, 94
Limoges, bishop of, 22, 23
Lisbon, 20
Louis VIII, 44
Louis IX, 44
Ludwig of Wittelsbach, 70
Luke, 23, 27, 37
Lusignan, see first names
Lüttich, 3

Macarius, 63
Macchabees, I, 28, 40
Madianites, 92
Magdeburg, 13
Magi, 51
Mahalec, 75, 81, 83
Mahaut, 30
Malik-al-Adil Seif-ed-Dîn, 30
Malik-al-Afdal, 52
Malik-al-Aschraf, 52, 69
Malik-al-Aziz, 52
Malik-al-Kamil Mohammed, 30, 31, 83, 89
Malik-al-Moadden Isa, 39
Malta, count of, 91
Malta, knights of, 17
Mamelukes, 66
mangonels, 44
Mantua, bishop of, 29
Margaret of France, 12
Marie of Cyprus, 70
Marie of Montferrat, 12, 52, 68
Maron, St., 78
Maronites, 78
Marshal of the Hospitallers, 42, 43, 93
Marshal of the Templars, 39, 87
Marshal of the Teutonic House, 65, 91
Master of the Hospitallers, 13, 68, 74, 90, 93, 95

Master of the Templars, 39, 87
Master of the Teutonic House, 65, 91
Matthew, 32, 69
Matthew, count of Apulia, 62
Mecca, 45, 50
Mechlin, 32
Medes, 79, 82
Medzabaro, John, Catholicos, 63
Melchiseraph, 52
Melisende, 17
Meran, duke of, 12, 13
Methodius, 50
Milan, archbishop of, 61
Milo, count of Bar, 29, 30
Milon, bishop-elect of Beauvais, 42
Milly, *see* first names
Miralis, 52
Mohammed, 37, 50, 89
Mohammedans, 30, 90; law of, 37
Monophysites, 78, 79
Monothelitism, 78
Montagu, *see* first names
Monte Cassino, 29
Montferrat, *see* first names
Montréal, 45
Moses, 83, 92
Münster, bishop of, 13, 19; diocese, 21

Nahr Litani, 16
Namur, 3
Nanteuil, 42
Naplouse, 63
Nazareth, 14
Neophorites, 78
Nestorian Church, 63
Nestorians, 79
Nevers, count of, 29, 30
Nicosia, archbishop of, 13, 22, 67, 93
Nile, 23, 24, 26, 31, 45, 46, 61, 74, 75, 76, 81, 84, 91; floods fields and helps defeat the crusaders, 84, 85
Nordhausen, 9
Nubians, 50, 77
Numbers, 83, 92

Ogle, M. B., 50
Old Man of the Mountains, 51
Oliver of Paderborn: preaches crusade in Cologne, 1; writes history of Fifth Crusade and on history of Holy Land, 1; birth and early life, 1; probably noble, 2; canon of Paderborn, 2; *magister*, teaches theology, 2; teaches in cathedral school, 2; at Paris in 1207, 2; receives small church in Epernay, 3; returns to Cologne, 3; preaches crusade in company with Dean of Bonn, 3; success as preacher, 3; attends Lateran Council, 3; arrives in Holy Land, 3; works of, 3, 4; designs tower, 6, 25; ignorant of Arabic, 7; makes very few classical allusions, 7; in favor of Pelagius, 46; his advice rejected, 84; returns to Germany, 9; confirmed as Bishop of Paderborn, 10; Cardinal-Bishop of Saint Sabina, 10; death, 10
Oliver, son of John Lackland, 30
Orontes, 82
Otto, bishop of Münster, 13, 19
Otto, bishop of Utrecht, 13
Otto of Brunswick, 2
Otto of Freising, 51
Otto of Meran, 12, 13

Paderborn, 1, 2, 9, 10
Palestine, 18, 58, 67, 75, 94
Paphas, 94
Paralipomenon II, 49
Paris, bishop of, 29
Passau, bishop of, 70, 84
Patriarch of Jerusalem, 14, 15, 16, 22, 26, 41
Paul the Deacon, 8
Pelagius, Cardinal-Legate, 3, 4, 12, 31, 34, 35, 40, 46, 53, 54, 61, 62, 63, 64, 66, 68, 70, 72, 74, 82, 83, 85, 87, 90, 95
Pelusium, 56
Persia, 75
Persians, 51, 71, 79, 82, 87
Peter, bishop of Raab, 13
Peter of Courtenay, 30
Peter of Montagu, 13, 68, 93
Peter of Nemours, bishop of Paris, 29
Petersheim, 20
petraries, 25
Petrus Comestor, 7, 8, 50
Pharaoh, 48, 57

INDEX

Philip Augustus, 42
Philip of Antioch, 63, 94
Philip of Naplouse, 68
Philip of Swabia, 2
Philip the Fair, 17
Phrygia, 95
Pilgrims' Castle (Athlit, Castle of the Son of God, Château Pélerin), 18, 19, 22, 48, 58, 67, 91
Pisa, 42, 46
Pisans, 40
plague in Christian camp, 32, 33
Plaisance of Gibelet, 51, 63, 68
Poitou, 43
Portugal, 21; king of, 21; queen of, 20, 21
Preceptor of the Teutonic House, 65
Prester John, 51, 70, 83
Prophetia Filii Agap, 49
Prophétie de Hannan, La, 49
Proverbs, 60, 71
Prussia, 18
Psalms, 11, 39, 43, 53, 64, 71, 81
Puiset, *see* first names

Quinti Belli Sacri Scriptores Minores, 20, 21, 49
Quintus Curtius, 7, 23

Raab, bishop of, 13
Raamses, 47, 48
Rahab, 70
Ralph de Mauléon, 44
Ralph de Merencourt, patriarch of Jerusalem, 14, 22, 26
Ranulf, earl of Chester, 39
Raymond, count of Tripoli, 51
Raymond of Palafolls, archbishop of Gerona, 29
Recordane, 14
Reggio, 61
Regnier, bishop of Bethlehem, 22
Renaud de Chatillon, 45
Rezzato, Albert, bishop of Brescia, 61
Rheims, archbishop of, 22, 23, 42
Rhodes, knights of, 17
Richard of Sainte-Suzanne, 42
Richard the Lion-Hearted, 31, 32
Rio Sado, 20

Robert, bishop of Bayeux, 13
Robert of Belmont, 65
Robert of Courçon, cardinal-bishop of St. Stephen, 29
Röhricht, R., 20, 21, 49, 70, 95
Roland, bishop of Faenza, 61
Romans, 31, 84, 95
Romans, Epistle to, 11, 49
Rosetta, 67, 76
Rupen-Raymond, 53, 63, 93
Russi, 79

Saarbrücken, count of, 23, 42
sackbuts, 24
Safita, 26, 53, 59, 82
Saida, 78
Saint James, Knights of, 20
Sakif Arnun, 16
Saladin, 14, 30, 31, 36, 45, 49, 50, 51, 53, 59, 64, 82
Salpi, bishop of, 29
Samaria, 35
Samson, 32
Sandakli, 95
San Germano, 10
Saphidin, 12, 30, 31, 36, 52, 53
Saphira, 60
Saracens, 14, 19, 20, 23, 24, 27, 28, 30, 31, 34, 36, 37, 39, 40, 41, 42, 43, 45, 50, 52, 53, 56, 57, 58, 59, 67, 69, 70, 72, 73, 76, 77, 80, 83, 90, 93, 94
Saramsah, 74, 75, 81
Sarepta, 16
Savary of Mauléon, 44
Saxony, duke of, 66
Schilwolde, Herdericus of, 9
Schwerin, count of, 9, 66
Scylla, 96
Scythopolis, 14
Selefke, 52
Seljuk, 69
Septala, Henry, archbishop of Milan, 61
Seraphus, 69, 82, 89
Sergius, 37
Setubal, 20
Shiites, 78
Siblia, 95
Sicily, king of, 49, 95

INDEX

Sidon, 4, 16
Sigurd, prince of Norway, 1
Silesia-Breslau, duke of, 13
Simon, count of Saarbrücken, 23
Son of God, Castle of, *see* Pilgrims' Castle
Sophonias, 96
Spain, 12, 20
Spatarians, 20
Stephanie, 52, 61
Strigonium, 13
Suetonius, 7, 82
surrender of crusaders, 89, 90
Sussex, 62
Sybille, 63
Symon, 75, 85
Syria, 35, 36, 45, 52, 67, 68, 82, 84, 94
Syrians, 79

Tabor, Mount, 15, 19, 48, 59; captured by crusaders, 16
Taki ed din, 82
Tanis, 47, 48, 56, 57, 58, 59, 65, 75, 85
Tarsus, 63, 93
Tartars, 83
Tell Hum, 15
Templars, 5, 16, 17, 18, 19, 20, 22, 25, 31, 33, 35, 38, 39, 40, 42, 46, 48, 51, 52, 53, 59, 65, 67, 68, 82, 85, 87, 91
Teutons (Teutonic Knights), 18, 22, 24, 29, 38, 40, 41, 43, 65, 66, 91
Thessalonica, 66
Thibaud, count of Champagne, 13
Thomas, bishop of Erlau, 13, 29
Thomas Magister, 19
Tiberias, 14, 49
Titus, 11
Tobias, 43, 60
Toron, 16, 36
tortoises, 54
Tortosa, 51, 53
Toucy, lord of, 30
Toulouse, count of, 44
Tower of David, *see* David
trebuchets, 25

Trier, 22
Tripoli, 17, 82; count of, 51, 53, 95
Tubania, 14
Turcomans, 93
Turcopoles, 73
Turkey, 95
Turks, 65, 67, 87, 88, 95
Turo, 90, 92
Tusculum, 16
Tyre, 16, 68

Uelmen, Henry of, 42
Ulrich of Andechs-Diessen, 70
Urraca, queen of Portugal, 21
Utrecht, 3; bishop of, 13; diocese, 21

Venetians, 40, 67
Venice, 46; doge of, 66
Verona, Council of, 4, 95
von Brokel, family, 9; Henry, 9

Waldemar, king of Denmark, 9, 66
Walter, lord of Caesarea, 41
Walter of Avesnes, 13, 17, 18
Walter of Berthout, 41, 42
Walter of Puiset, 30
Walter of Villebléon, 42
Walter IV of Brienne, 70
Welfs, 2
Wied, count of, 29, 43
William, archbishop of Bordeaux, 29
William, count of Holland, 20
William, earl of Arundel, 62
William of Beaumont, bishop of Angers, 29, 42
William of Chartres, 29, 68 (identical with William of Puiset)
William of Tyre, 8
Wisdom, Book of, 71, 92
Wittewierum, abbot of, 9

Yolanda Courtenay, 12

Zabel, 63
Zachary, 90; canticle of, 27
Zeitz, bishop of, 13
Ziani, Pietro, doge of Venice, 68